POEMS OF LOVE AND HATE

Books by Josephine Balmer

Sappho: Poems and Fragments
(Bloodaxe Books, 1992)

Classical Women Poets
(Bloodaxe Books, 1996)

(ed.) *Rearranging the World: an Anthology of Literature in Translation*
(British Centre for Literary Translation, 2001)

Catullus: Poems of Love and Hate
(Bloodaxe Books, 2004)

Chasing Catullus: poems, translations & transgressions
(Bloodaxe Books, 2004)

CATULLUS

POEMS OF LOVE
AND HATE

TRANSLATED BY
JOSEPHINE BALMER

BLOODAXE BOOKS

ISBN: 1 85224 645 6

First published 2004 by
Bloodaxe Books Ltd,
Highgreen,
Tarset,
Northumberland NE48 1RP.

www.bloodaxebooks.com
For further information about Bloodaxe titles
please visit our website or write to
the above address for a catalogue.

Bloodaxe Books Ltd acknowledges
the financial assistance of
Arts Council England, North East.

Cover printing by J. Thomson Colour Printers Ltd, Glasgow.

Printed in Great Britain by
Cromwell Press Ltd, Trowbridge, Wiltshire.

...chance readers of my fools' verse, my book,
don't delay, please, take a closer look...

CONTENTS

INTRODUCTION

my satisfaction will be longest: this

Catullus the Survivor

Despite his own firm belief in the immortality of his poetry, Catullus' work escaped eternal oblivion by a hair's breadth. Until the 14th century, only one of his poems, a marriage-hymn, survived in a 9th century anthology of classical poets. Then, seemingly out of the blue, a manuscript containing 116 poems – probably Catullus' complete œuvre – turned up in Verona, the poet's own home town. This manuscript, apparently written in France in the late 12th century,[1] disappeared again a few years later, this time for good. But all was not lost; it had already been copied – possibly for the Italian poet Petrarch[2] – and then recopied again. The text we now have is based on three surviving second- or third-hand copies, each one packed with textual errors and savagely emended by scholars over the centuries, but similar enough to lead them to believe that the words on the page are as close as we might hope to get to Catullus' own – a miracle of literary tenacity.

It is not difficult to see why Catullus might have needed one. Alongside his lyrical love poetry, revered for its direct passion and fierce intensity, there was also his array of picaresque and often unsavoury characters – the elegant and articulate Suffenus who wrote poetry like a 'goat-milker', Egnatius who cleaned his teeth in the alarming 'Spanish' manner, Rufus with his goat-like arm-pits or Arrius with his irritating habit of pronouncing his haitches – who might not appeal to all. And as well as his taste for salacious tales, there were also Catullus' dense scholarly and literary references, which could alienate readers once their context had been lost or forgotten. After being revered, even parodied, in the early classical world, mentioned by his fellow Latin poets Propertius, Ovid, Horace, Juvenal and especially Martial, read by both the elder and the younger Pliny, Catullus' verse seems to have fallen out of fashion sometime in the 2nd century AD, with only a few brief references in subsequent writers. As Goold has pointed out, among the hundreds of literary quotations scrawled on the walls

---

[1] So claimed an accompanying Latin verse, allegedly by the Italian poet Benvenuto Campesani (for a text and translation see Goold, 2001: 29).

[2] See Fordyce, 1961: xxvii & Wiseman, 1985: 211.

of Pompeii, there is not one word of Catullus.[3] And then, when the classical world collapsed, the custodianship of its literary works passed into the hands of medieval monasteries, whose monks made copies of the texts they wanted to preserve; Catullus' scurrilous lampoons and scatological, often downright obscene imagery (using language rarely found outside scrawled graffiti), was hardly well-placed to convince the Christian Church of his worth.

Nevertheless, someone somewhere was reading his works, keeping them alive. We know, for instance, that around the turn of the 5th century AD, St Jerome, the Latin translator of the Old Testament, included Catullus in his *Chronicle*, an account of historical events and dates. Similarly, in the 7th century, Bishop Isidore of Spain quoted a few tags of Catullus in an etymological encyclopaedia. Of the poetry's progress through the so-called Dark Ages into the light of the Renaissance, however, hardly anything is known. Yet its reputation was such that its rediscovery was enthusiastically received, at least in Europe; despite the corruption of the text, and the density of its often obscure literary allusions, European poets took Catullus' verse to heart, praising its passionate sensuality, translating it, imitating it and interpreting it with gusto (including the theory that Catullus' sparrow poems represented an obscene allegory that could hardly be explained 'with modesty intact').[4]

It wasn't all plain sailing. A complete Latin text of Catullus' verse was not published in rather more conservative England until 1684, and then it took another 100 years for a complete translation to appear. Even then, its translator, John Nott, while claiming that he hadn't glossed over any of the poems, 'however disgusting to our sensations and repugnant to our natures', paraphrased much of Catullus' more colloquial language.[5] In the 19th century, Victorian sensibilities might have been moved by Catullus' elegy for a brother fallen in a foreign land or titillated by his counting up of a sweetheart's kisses, but they were hardly likely to be gratified by Catullus' disrespect to his colonial superior ('that mouth-fucker praetor') or his scabrous attacks on military leaders of the day (the 'chief bumboys' Julius Caesar and Pompey), let alone his passion for his 'honeyboy' Juventius alongside his mistress Lesbia.

By the eve of the 20th century, things had hardly improved. In

---

[3] See note on No.86 [Catullus 4]; Goold, 2001: 9.

[4] Angelo Poliziano, *Miscellanies*, 1.6. translated by Julia Haig Gaisser (2001: xxv). For the sparrow poems see Nos.3 & 4 [Catullus 2 & 3].

[5] John Nott, *The Poems of Caius Valerius Catullus in English Verse*, 1795, quoted by Gaisser (2001: xxxvii).

1894, Sir Richard Burton's apparently plain-speaking translations were bowdlerised after his death by his wife, with the horrified Lady Burton substituting asterisks for all offending words (rather depleting the opening line of No.36 [Catullus 16]). Similarly, at the beginning of the Swinging Sixties, C.J. Fordyce's otherwise comprehensive edition omitted 32 poems which did not 'lend themselves to comment in English', even if an anonymous review by one of Fordyce's own students at Glasgow University wailed in despair: '*Tropic of Cancer* has been published in vain, Lady Chatterley has tripped naked through the bluebells to no avail'.[6] To such commentators Catullus seemed to have a split personality, on the one hand a witty, if passionate, gentleman and scholar, on the other a depraved pervert whom it would be best, not least in his own interests, to ignore. But Catullus the survivor couldn't be dismissed so easily. At the beginning of the 21st century, with a wealth of recent scholarship to draw on, including studies of Latin demotic as well as of ancient sexuality and society,[7] the poet's darker, more disreputable doppelgänger seems closer – and funnier – than ever.

Catullus the Man

So much for the historical survival of the text, but what of Caius Valerius Catullus the historical man? Hardly surprisingly, evidence is slight and over-reliant on the poems themselves. With no reliable external evidence, and no reference in his own poetry to any historical event beyond Caesar's invasion of Britain in 55 BC – and possibly Calvus' prosecution of Vatinius in 54 BC [8] – many commentators have concluded that the poet must have died late in 54 BC. Citing a line from Ovid as additional evidence of Catullus' early death,[9] his birth is then back-dated to around 84 BC. Catullus' poetry, however, whilst stuffed with allusion to contemporary figures as well as to literature and mythology, is for the most part historically imprecise and vague, as Charles Martin points out, only referring to historical events when they impinge upon his own consciousness.[10] Besides, Catullus lived in dangerous times, when

---

[6] Preface to Fordyce, 1961; review quoted by Wiseman, 1985: 242.

[7] See Adams (2002), Cantarella (2002), Fitzgerald (2000), Krostenko (2001) & Williams (1999).

[8] See Nos.9, 91 & 54 [Catullus 11, 29 & 53].

[9] *Amores*, 3. 9.61. St Jerome's *Chronicle* dates Catullus to 87-57 BC – dates disproved by No.9 [Catullus 11].

[10] Martin, 1992: 41.

the personal power of men such as Caesar and Pompey was beginning to threaten the stability of the republican state, leading eventually to civil war in 49 BC; even someone as sharp-tongued as Catullus might know when it was time to keep quiet. Indeed, one modern study has even suggested that, far from dying tragically young, pen in hand, Catullus lived to a ripe old age, writing not poetry but comic theatrical farce.[11]

Nevertheless, the poems do provide some invaluable information about Catullus' life and circle. It seems unarguable that he was born in Verona, in what was then the province of Cisalpine Gaul, to a wealthy family; Suetonius recounts that the poet's father was a friend of Julius Caesar, the most powerful man of his day, although Catullus' own vicious attacks on the general were rather less cordial.[12] Apart from Caesar, the poems mention a string of illustrious and distinguished contemporaries including the orator Cicero, the historian Cornelius Nepos, to whom Catullus' work is dedicated, the orator and poet Licinius Calvus, apparently Catullus' great friend, as well as the general Pompey, Caesar's ally and later adversary. Although most of Catullus' *dramatis personae* can be identified only tentatively, if at all, some provide valuable clues. For instance, Catullus' rants against his hated praetor, Memmius, on whose staff, we learn, he had served in Bithynia, help date events in the poet's life; Caius Memmius was governor of Bithynia in 57 BC, when Catullus would have accompanied him east, returning home in 56 BC, as one of his most famous poems celebrates.[13]

Despite this one instance of public office, however, Catullus' poetry is surprisingly unconcerned with Roman public life; while on the one hand viciously satirising Caesar, Pompey, or their grasping, spendthrift cohort Mamurra, the poems seem inured to the lure of the so-called *cursus honorum*, the rungs of office which ambitious wealthy young Romans climbed on their way to political power. Indeed a few explicitly reject the path of public advancement, along with its requisite sycophancy and mutual back-scratching – although there remains a lingering suspicion that this isn't so much moral outrage as the enraged indignation of the excluded, even if by their own fastidiousness.[14] Typically, though, the poet's one recorded visit to the Forum, the Roman seat of political as well as commercial power, is to inspect his friend Varus' latest girl

[11] Wiseman, 1985: 183-89.
[12] *Julius Caesar*, 73. See Nos.91 & 95-97 [Catullus 29, 57, 93 & 54].
[13] See Nos.88-9 [Catullus 10 & 28]; No.87 [Catullus 31].
[14] Nos.89 & 98 [Catullus 28 & 52].

– and to embarrass himself by being caught out boasting about non-existent spoils from his time in the East.[15]

Catullus the Lover

If not directly political, the poems are certainly passionate, often using the language of public life in a private, personal context, much as Sappho used the language of military warfare for the love between women.[16] As with Sappho, whom Catullus greatly admired and imitated, the intensity and directness of the Roman poet's love poems have reached out to their readers over the centuries, seemingly sprung direct 'from life',[17] so much so that, like the endless speculation surrounding Sappho's sexuality, scholarly debate from antiquity onwards has often centred on the "real" identity of Catullus' mistress Lesbia.

As early as the second century AD, curiosities were aroused by Apuleius' assertion that 'Lesbia's' real name was 'Clodia'.[18] Soon after Catullus' rediscovered text was published in the Renaissance, Lesbia was firmly identified with Clodia Metelli, one of the most infamous women in Rome. Wealthy, beautiful and sophisticated, with an admirable disregard for Roman conventions about the behaviour of respectable women (a 'two-penny Clytemnestra',[19] as her disillusioned lover Caelius called her), Clodia was the half-sister of the populist politician P. Clodius Pulcher.[20] Around 79 BC, she married her older cousin, Q. Metellus Celer, who became governor of Cisalpine Gaul in 62 BC. Nevertheless Clodia scandalised Rome with her string of affairs, so much so that when Metellus died in 59 BC the word in the city was that Clodia had poisoned him. After his death, she took as her lover M. Caelius Rufus, a protégé of Cicero, much to the orator's horror. When the affair ended in 56 BC, she accused Caelius of attempting to poison her, although he was successfully defended by Cicero, whose surviving speech, packed full of innuendo about Clodia's apparently shameless adventuring, provides valuable, if hardly unbiased, evidence. Little was subse-

---

[15] No.88 [Catullus 10].
[16] See in particular Nos.12 & 24 [Catullus 87 & 109]. On Sappho see Balmer, 1992: 20-23.
[17] Lyne, 1980:20.
[18] *Apologia*, 10.
[19] Caelius, *Orations*, 23.
[20] Clodius was also the man caught hiding in woman's clothes at the woman-only festival of the Bona Dea celebrated by Caesar's wife Pompeia in 62 BC; at the subsequent trial, Caesar refused to testify against Clodius but divorced Pompeia on the grounds that Caesar's wife 'must be above suspicion'.

quently heard of her although several years later in 45 BC, an equally shameless Cicero made approaches about buying her riverside house. The lady was not for selling.[21]

What excited scholars most about Clodia's identification with Lesbia was the seeming ease with which her biographical details could be slotted in to Catullus' poems – or vice versa; the fact that Catullus' Lesbia was also married; Metellus' connection with Cisalpine Gaul, Catullus' home; the mention of a 'Caelius' and a 'Rufus' in Catullus' poetry. Certainly, in No.14 [Catullus 79], Catullus puns on the name of Lesbia's brother – Pulcher or 'pretty' – the same cognomen as Clodius, and a joke Cicero had also used of him. Catullus' insinuation in the poem that Lesbia committed incest with her brother has also excited interest; Cicero had implied as much of Clodia and Clodius in his defence of Caelius.[22] However, as modern studies have been quick to point out, Clodius had more than one sister, all of whom, under Roman custom, would have shared the same name.[23]

Yet, as other recent commentators note, literature isn't necessarily biography, and poetry, however direct and apparently sincere, cannot be read as such.[24] Even Lesbia's name is a highly artificial literary joke, playing with its connections with Sappho, renowned in ancient Rome for her highly-charged emotional power, rather than any modern connotation of 'Sapphism' (in fact, 'Lesbia', in line with Catullus' love for low sexual innuendo, as well as high literary learning, was more likely to be a pun on the Greek verb *lesbiazein* which the Athenian comic playwright Aristophanes used of women expert at fellatio).[25] Charles Martin has argued that it is easier to think of Lesbia not as a real person but a theme running through Catullus' poetry, 'an emblem, abstracted and idealised…the projection of his erotic expectations and disappointments'.[26] Nevertheless, it is precisely this complex artistry which continues to excite our curiosity, ensuring that the love affair, whether fictional or not, has became one of the most closely-examined in literature.

---

[21] Cicero, *Letters to Atticus*, 12. 42.2.

[22] Cicero, *Caelius*, 36.

[23] Wiseman, 1969: 50-60. Charles Martin has pointed out that it is precisely this custom of naming women firstly after their father's and then their husband's family that might have led to the adoption of a lover's pseudonym, freeing her from 'patriarchal domination' and providing 'a new secret identity shared only with the lover.' (1992: 43).

[24] Godwin, 1999: 12-16.

[25] For example Aristophanes, *Wasps*, 1346.

[26] Martin, 1992: 48.

Also under close scrutiny over the centuries, of course, has been Catullus' own sexuality. As with Sappho, the apparent bisexuality of his verse has often confounded commentators, while its constant threat of physical violence, notably male homosexual rape, has regularly appalled. Recent studies, though, have pointed to the difference in ancient and modern male sexual consciousness.[27] In a pre-Christian Roman moral value system, what mattered was not the gender of a partner but the nature of the sexual act; in a culture founded on conquest, which measured social standing through military prowess, the insistence on domination extended to the sexual milieu, as did the shameful taboo of subjection. As Catullus' poems reveal over and over again, to be penetrated was to be humiliated. In No.42 [Catullus 15], for instance, we learn that betrayed husbands or lovers could take revenge by inserting objects into their rivals' anuses, as Catullus threatens Aurelius. Similarly, one of Catullus' most common threats to his enemies is of *irrumatio*, a word which has no real English equivalent but referred to an enforced act of fellatio, or 'mouth-fucking', interestingly the inverse to our 'cock-sucker'. For whereas in English the passive partner is insulted, in Latin the emphasis is all on the aggressor.[28]

Such poems – and such threats – have led some readers to feel repulsed not just by Catullus' verse but by what they perceive to be the poet's character. Harold Nicolson, for example, reading Lord Hailsham's translations in *The Spectator* in January 1957, declared the Roman poet 'vindictive, venomous, and full of obscene malice'. Yet for the most part, we might agree rather with the classical scholar Richard Jenkyns, who concluded instead that, despite hearing a great deal about Catullus' various emotions, 'in the end we have hardly any idea of what he was really like'.[29] For while we might be outraged at his obscenities, enchanted by his courtships, amused at his jokes, the man himself remains elusive, slips through our fingers again and again.

Part of the problem, perhaps, is Catullus' diversity as poet, one moment speaking the language of learned Alexandrian scholarship, the next the language of the Roman gutter; one moment presenting

---

[27] Wiseman, 1985: 10-14. See also Cantarella (2002); Williams (1999).

[28] Cicero's accusation that Clodia arranged for two of her henchmen to rape a reluctant lover (*Caelius*, 71) is interesting here; whether Clodia is Lesbia, it reveals the Roman link between the infliction of punishment, the exertion of power and homosexual rape.

[29] Harold Nicolson, *Diaries and Letters*, 1945-62, quoted in Wiseman, 1985: 241; Jenkyns, 1982: 84.

us with a risqué two-line tag about some loathed contemporary figure, the next with a four-hundred line mythological epic; one moment tenderly kissing Lesbia, the next threatening Furius and Aurelius with homosexual rape. The reader has to deal with not just one Catullus or even two, good and bad, but several. In this context, his verse can be seen not as personal outpouring, a record of the poet's life or character, but more as performance, with the 'Catullus' mentioned over and over again in the texts an actor in the poem's own drama. Even Catullus' long, inner monologues are highly artificial, echoing the dramatic monologues of Greek tragedy or, as Godwin has pointed out, the indecisive lover of ancient comedy, revealing a fluidity of voice and stance with an often ambiguous moral conclusion.[30] As Catullus himself reminds Furius and Aurelius in No.36 [Catullus 16], poetry should never be confused with the poet. We might add that what matters is not the man but the poem itself, however complicated, however diverse, however obscene.

Catullus the Poet

Catullus wasn't alone in his poetic course. He appears to have belonged to a group of young poets, whom Cicero referred to as *neoterics* or 'the new poets',[31] not so much a movement, perhaps, but a loose unit of friends which included Calvus, Cinna, Cornificius and Caecilius, all mentioned in Catullus' verse, all apparently influenced by the wealth of Greek literature that had been filtering back to Rome since its conquest of Greece in the early 2nd century BC. Catullus' own poetry includes a variety of intertextual references to Greek genres, from the inspiring imagery of Homeric epic to the jokes of Aristophanic comedy.[32] By reading the 7th century lyric poet Archilochus, Catullus learnt the art of writing witty, insouciant, seductive verse; while in Hipponax's satirical lampoons, he found new metres, notably the scazon or 'limping iambic'. He found new metres, too, in Sappho, as well as translating – and transforming – her meltingly erotic imagery.[33]

But it was the so-called Hellenistic or Alexandrian poets of the

---

[30] Godwin, 1999: 123. See Nos.7 & 22 [Catullus 8 & 76].
[31] *Letters to Atticus*, 7.2.1.
[32] For example the imagery of No.31 [Catullus 60] echoes that of *Iliad* 16. 33-35, while the 'cold writing' joke of No.57 [Catullus 44] is found in Aristophanes' *Acharnians* 138-40.
[33] See Nos.5, 9 & 83 [Catullus 51, 11 & 68a] and discussion p.20 below.

mid-3rd century BC, who most fired Catullus and his contemporaries. From poets such as Callimachus, whom, like Sappho, Catullus translated,[34] the Roman neoterics learnt the art of the minor epic, of concise epigrams and occasional verse, verse which celebrated not the great achievements of nations and armies but "small" everyday events, captured, nevertheless, in the language of high literary artifice, with the emphasis on scholarly learning and verbal dexterity. Over and over again, Catullus echoes Hellenistic poems in his own, over-writing them like lines on a palimpsest: the personification of an inanimate object, a door or a boat; the celebration of erotic inter-ludes; the mourning for a dead pet; the playful emphasis on the art of poetry-writing – and its power.[35] And from Hellenistic poetry, as from classical, he adapted a new metre, the Phalaecian or hen-decasyllable – a metre he used not only to praise the dedication and skill of Alexandrian poets, but to poke fun at the 'inflated' art of the old school, both Greek and Roman, defining his new move-ment, as is so often the case, by exclusion.[36]

Nevertheless Catullus was steeped in Roman tradition too. And by lending a Roman flavour to the Greek forms he borrowed, he gave his poetry its unique edge. Certainly Catullus and his fellow-poets seem to have employed an array of Latin aesthetic value-terms almost as a private poetic language. These terms, including *lepidus/illepidus* (of mental agility), *venustus/invenustus* (of sexual desirability) and *facetus/infacetus* (of verbal wit and dexterity), created a complex patterning of peer approval – and disapproval – forming what Brian Krostenko has called 'the language of social perform-ance'.[37] There were other idiomatic expressions, too, such as the unusual plural *deliciae*, which Catullus used mostly as a term of endearment in the sense of 'pet' or 'darling' (but which, as Cicero notes, also had overtones of sexual dalliance).[38] Important here, too, was the repeated use of diminutives, a form derived from Roman colloquial speech, but employed by Catullus to ironic literary effect, as in the description of Thallus' effeminacy in No.63 [Catullus 25].[39] Most of all, though, Catullus took the Alexandrian ideal of blend-ing high and low art to new levels, interweaving his Greek literary allusions with demotic Latin, inventing new words such as *fututiones*

---

[34] See No.82 & Endpiece [Catullus 65 & 116].
[35] See Nos.85, 86, 25, 4 & 53 [Catullus 67, 4, 32, 3 & 50].
[36] See Nos.36, 55 & 61 [Catullus 16, 14 & 42].
[37] Krostenko, 2001.
[38] See, for example, Nos.4, 25 & 47 [Catullus 3, 32 & 6]; Cicero, *Caelius*, 44.
[39] See Goold, 2001: 6.

('fuck-fuckings') – a deliberately learned-sounding polysyllable from the coarse verb *futuere*, infusing his obscene and often scatological imagery with the Alexandrian ideals of 'elegance, wit, grace, brevity and charm'.[40]

A key text here is No.9 [Catullus 11], addressed to two Catullan regulars, Furius and Aurelius. The poem starts with a typically ironical address to the poet's *comites* or 'close friends' (the pair are elsewhere viciously attacked), a word with the peculiarly Roman connotation of colleagues on the staff of a provincial governor. There follows a characteristically Alexandrian list of geographical locations, embellished with suitably learned compound adjectives. For a Roman audience each one would have conjured up recent military campaigns in the east. The list culminates in real time, with an ironic reference to Caesar's successes in Gaul and Britain in 55 BC. Then – at last – we reach the point of the poem; never mind traversing faraway territories, all that Furius and Aurelius need to do is step across Rome and take a message to the poet's girl, presumably Lesbia – a message dryly described as *non bona dicta*, 'not quite so kind'. This bathetic understatement moves into focus in the next stanza as Catullus launches a sexually-charged attack on his lover in the language of Roman street slang; after being unfaithful to the poet with a string of *moechi*, an abusive word for adulterer, Lesbia, characterised as sexually energetic but emotionally cold, has left her partners exhausted and drained, in the Latin idiom *ilia rumpens*, 'breaking their balls'.

After the shock of this coarse abuse, the poem's tone changes again, ending with a beautiful, delicate simile almost certainly based on one of Sappho's wedding hymns; as a result of his lover's unfaithfulness, the poet's love has been destroyed, like a flower on the edge of a meadow cut down by a passing plough. But whereas Sappho compares a girl's lost virginity to a hyacinth trampled underfoot by shepherds, here it is male love which is the victim of a woman's casual destruction: male physical violence has became female emotional indifference.[41]

Catullus' gender reversal is central to his poetic persona, both as a poet of love and as a poet of hate. For Catullus' anger at Lesbia,

---

[40] No.25 [Catullus 32]; Godwin, 1999: 11.
[41] Sappho, fragment 105c (see also Balmer, 1992: 22 & 58). To Godwin, however, Catullus' rewriting of Sappho is a counterbalance of the poem's earlier list of male colonial conquests, ironically revealing how 'the male who could stride the Alps is shown at the end as a lover whose love can be destroyed simply by a touch' (1999: 128).

here and elsewhere, seems born out of humiliation; the poet's apparently unreciprocated passion for an uncaring Lesbia has made him the passive partner – the ultimate taboo for a male Roman lover. Other differences are equally telling; gone is Sappho's exploration – and celebration – of woman's distinctive emotional experience, gone is the Greek delineation between defined male and female worlds, male and female consciousness.[42] In Catullus, there is only one world, one consciousness: male. Even his poetry's single reference to female pudenda (*cunnus*) is used in a male context, as a comic description of Aemilius' grotesque mouth.[43] No wonder Lesbia looked elsewhere.

Catullus the Translation

In the past, poems such as these understandably caused Lady Burton et al the most difficulties. Today's more liberal sensibilities might not find it necessary to bowdlerise or censor the text when writing – or publishing – English versions. What troubles instead is the issue of tone and register. How, for example, can we translate Catullus' one use of *cunnus* or his many utterances of the "low" Latin verb *futuere* and its derivatives? What sort of obscenity are we dealing with in Latin? What sort of outrage, if any, would it have caused in its original context and where can we gauge that scale of taboo in contemporary English? For *cunnus*, at least, we have an expert witness; in a private letter, Cicero apparently refers to the same word, a word, he says, that should never pass the lips.[44] Recent linguistic studies, such as J.N. Adams' breathtakingly exhaustive *The Latin Sexual Vocabulary*, are also indispensable here, examining every known occurrence and context of a string of words which, in the past, would make only the briefest of appearances in standard dictionaries, comparing and contrasting synonyms and euphemisms to build up a rounded picture of contemporary Latin usage.

Adams' work has opened up a wealth of knowledge about Catullus' use of sexual idiom, revealing the hidden innuendo and double

---

[42] In No.5 [Catullus 51]. Catullus also subtly changes and transforms Sappho fragment 31, making Sappho's illusory verse far more definite, focusing not so much on the generic symptoms of desire but on the poet's own jealousy of his rival for Lesbia's attention and affection. And whereas Sappho's man only listens to the woman, Catullus also looks at (*spectat*) Lesbia; on the other hand, Sappho's woman both laughs and speaks but Lesbia isn't permitted a word.

[43] No.69 [Catullus 97].

[44] Cicero, *Letters to His Friends*, 9.22.

entendres in some of the most seemingly innocent of expressions, allowing us to share the jokes, possibly for the first time in two thousand years: in No.97 [Catullus 54], for example, the reference to Otho's small head can, with Adams' help, be unravelled as a sexual pun; Latin *caput*, it seem, had a similar meaning to our 'knob-head'. Again, we learn that the image of Fabullus becoming 'all nose' in No.45 [Catullus 13] probably had a more obscene meaning, with Latin *nasus* employed as a sexual metaphor, rather like our 'horn'.[45]

Gradually, in the process of translation, other jokes, too, began to reveal themselves, like colour seeping into a black and white film; Catullus' play on *notus* 'well-known' and *nothus* 'bastard' in No.14 [Catullus 79], for example, or his teasing pun on *catulus*, 'a little dog' and his own name in No.61 [Catullus 42]. My aim throughout was to provide English versions which reflected these new understandings, which brought Catullus' humour back to life, making it as enjoyable in the 21st century AD as it was in the 1st century BC. No.26 [Catullus 41], for instance, in which Catullus berates Ameana, a big-nosed prostitute, for her steep prices, ends with a pun on *aes*, or 'bronze', used metaphorically here of both money and a mirror; Ameana's greed, the poet implies, demands the former, but her plainness requires the latter. Fortunately this is a joke English easily allows:

> she needs a brass mirror above the bed
> so she can reflect on her own ceiling.

No.25 [Catullus 32] has another typically playful ending; after begging Ipsitilla for an afternoon assignation, Catullus puns on *pransus*, a military metaphor which originally meant 'having breakfasted' but, as troops never march on an empty stomach, came to mean 'ready for action'. In addition, the poet is *satur*, 'full' and *pertundo tunicamque palliumque*, literally 'boring through both cloak and tunic'. In my version this became:

> you see I've eaten, had my fill,
> yet still my lunch-box is bulging.

Finding English equivalents, though, can be tricky. Sexual idiom, in particular, changes so quickly – witness the now obsolete 1940s slang 'block' for having sex – rendering one generation's hilarious pun incomprehensible to the next, requiring as much of a scholarly

---

[45] Adams, 2002: 35 & 98.

gloss as one of Catullus' own.[46] Gauging levels of public reception and outrage can also be a difficult and complicated task; the near-riot caused when George Bernard Shaw's Eliza Doolittle first said 'bloody' on the London stage in 1914 might have seemed incredible to the audiences of John Osborne's *Look Back in Anger* 40 years or so later. Nevertheless, four decades after 'block' had passed out of common usage as a sexual idiom, the verb was still banned from use in headlines by some British provincial newspapers. Slang, too, can very easily appear dated, as we see in some earlier colloquial American translations of Catullus.[47] In such circumstances, the translator needs to be considered and thoughtful, putting as much energy into understanding their translation's contemporary context, its impact on its target culture, as they might expend on understanding the intricate web of culturally-specific references in its source text.[48] That said, it is also important not to be afraid of having fun, as Catullus himself certainly did, using up-to-the-minute slang words and colloquialisms alongside antiquated learned jargon, mixing in neologisms and foreign words, attacking sensibilities, shocking with the new. After all, if the original takes risks, then so, too, should the translation.

Nevertheless, there is still the danger of 'over-translating', that a version's new-found frankness, as Julia Haig Gaisser has commented, might lead to 'exaggerating or outdoing Catullus himself'. For, as with any other poet, Catullus' robust language cannot be considered a separate entity to his verse, to be expunged or embellished with impunity.[49] Rather, it is indivisible from his poetic art; translating the "obscene" poems becomes exactly the same act as translating the love poems for Lesbia. There is the same need to capture the fluidity and pace of the original Latin, its wit and elegance, the concision of Catullus' complex verbal constructions, his

---

[46] For example, an English joke dating from the Second World War, in which a man rushes into a shop: 'Quick, I need some salt!' 'Do you want a block?' asks the attractive female assistant. 'I haven't got time for that now,' replies the man, 'my chimney's on fire.' The pun relies on three pivots: the slang 'block' for having sex, the fact that salt used to be sold in blocks and the use of such blocks of salt in putting out chimney fires.

[47] For example some, but by no means all, of Frank O. Copley's lively, colloquial 1957 versions can now seem dated.

[48] For instance, when considering Catullus' use of *futuere* Jesse Sheidlower's *The F*** Word: A Complete History* (1999) proved invaluable.

[49] Gaisser, 2001: xxxviii. Besides, as John Godwin has noted, some of Catullus most obscene poems, such as No.71 [Catullus 80], a toe-curling tale of Gellius' acts of fellatio, don't contain a single Latin obscenity (1999: 196).

assured use of chiasmus, anaphora, asyndeton, litotes and other rhetorical figures, the melodic jingle of his internal and end rhymes, the intricate semantic patterning, the metrical innovations. To this end, as with my previous translations of classical verse, I used a syllabic verse form to echo Catullus' throughout, standing in for the "syllable value" (long or short) form of classical versification. I also employed end rhymes, both full and half, to echo the poems' aural tone and pitch, alongside their wit. For what defines Catullus' poetic art most of all is not just a sense of mischief, but a sense of music.

And yet, as we have seen, Catullus' violently-charged sexuality, however teasing, can still disturb. Just as early translators of Sappho's Greek changed the gender of her pronouns, so translators of Catullus changed his young male beloved, Juventius, to the female 'Crastinia'.[50] And just as Catullus subverted Sappho's essentially female poetics in his cross-gendered versions, so there might have been a temptation here, as a 21st century woman, to subvert Catullus' male Roman sensibilities, overwriting them with an implicit, if playful, challenge to his imagery of domination and submission.[51] Certainly in the past women translators do not appear to have been particularly drawn to Catullus; of the 75 or so translators whose work is anthologised in Julia Haig Gaisser's *Catullus in English*, only five are women (and none of these have attempted more than a few selections). However, it seemed to me that the poetry was already quite subversive enough. And perhaps, as a woman, I could not take his belligerent posturing too seriously. But then neither, one suspects, did Catullus.

Catullus the book

Where this translation might have strayed, at least in some eyes, is in its treatment of Catullus' collection as a whole. Ever since his poetry reappeared in 14th century Verona, a controversy has raged over whether the manuscript represented Catullus' collection of poetry as he himself had ordered it, with scholarly opinion swinging from side to side. The Verona text is neatly ordered by metre, divided into three clear sections; the first 60 poems written in a variety of lyric metres, including scazons and hendecasyllables,

---

[50] See Balmer, 1992: 13 *ff*; Gaisser, 2001: xxxix.
[51] See, for example, Suzanne Jill Levine's *The Subversive Scribe* (Graywolf Press, 1991) on her transformations of male Latin American writers.

a section known as the polymetric poems. The second section contains eight long poems, ranging from around 50 to 400 lines, again all in a variety of metres. Finally, the third section contains 48 short epigrams in elegiac couplets. All subsequent Latin editions, from the 15th century to the present day, have followed this pattern, keeping the poems in the text's original order.

Across these three sections, poems are placed not by subject-matter but randomly scattered, with the poet in love with Lesbia one minute, hating her the next, while swooning after Juventius or abusing Aurelius or Furius in between. In the past, commentators looking to unravel a biographical sequence in the Lesbia poems, for instance, have tried to reorder them in supposed chronological order, with No.5 [Catullus 51] seen as Catullus' first verse to her and the vicious missive of No.9 [Catullus 11] his last.[52] More recently, though, scholars have preferred to eschew a biographical approach and concentrate instead on uncovering a clear poetic purpose – not to mention Catullus' own hand – in the text's seemingly random order.[53]

Such arguments are both fascinating and compelling; the collection opens, for example, with Catullus' gift of verse being offered to his friend Cornelius Nepos and ends with the poet's gift of verse being rejected by his enemy Gellius. Attempts to show a chiasmic, or symmetrical, arrangement for the section of long poems, too, are equally convincing, as is the argument that the three sections of the book could represent the three volumes, each one collected on a separate papyrus roll, of Catullus' original publication. And yet, after so long a passage of time and so dark a history, it would seem a second miracle if Catullus' book had survived intact, if not just his poems, but the way in which he himself had ordered them had somehow remained unaltered after 1500 years – and with so obscured a history in between. The neat metrical divisions, too, seem to echo the manner of later classical anthologists. A.L. Wheeler, for instance, has concluded not only that the collection as we have it could not have been put together until after Catullus' death, but that its arrangement has 'greatly obscured the poet's own purposes and methods'. John Godwin's recent edition is more circumspect, noting that the poems do seem to have had been ordered with care, even if we can't be sure who did the ordering.[54]

---

[52] For example Quinn, 1996: 125.

[53] Wiseman, 1985: 136.

[54] A.L. Wheeler, *Catullus and the Traditions of Ancient Poetry*, cited by Charles Martin, 1992: 33-34; Godwin, 1999: 19.

Bearing such views in mind, my decision here to change the Renaissance order of the poems in my book of translations is based on two considerations: firstly that this volume covers the shorter poems only, omitting the longer mythological and ritual verse (to appear in a subsequent, separate volume). But secondly, and most importantly, on a desire for the poetry to be as accessible as possible, as enjoyable – but most of all as funny – to those with no prior knowledge of Latin or of the poet. To this end, I decided to group the poems by theme, as I had done with my previous translation of Sappho. For instance, poems concerning Roman political life, such as Catullus' attacks on Julius Caesar, come in close proximity to each other, as do his lampoons on turgid poets, minimising the need for repetitive explanations and to help fix an impression of the poems' diverse cast of characters.

The addition of titles was also important here, providing brief introductory explanations of the poem's context or addressee. For those curious to know more, footnotes to the translations appear at the end of the book, although these are designed to form a complementary rather than essential commentary on the English versions (a list of proper names can be found in a separate glossary). For as with all translations of verse, the poetry, with all its beauty, obscenity, and above all its wit, must ultimately speak for itself in English as it does in Latin.

Perhaps most controversially of all, the Lesbia poems, both those which actually bear her name and those which are traditionally believed to have been written about her, have been ordered neither in the random order in which they appear in the original manuscript nor in the chronological sequence subsequently ascribed to them by some commentators. Nevertheless the aim here was for them to spark off each other, giving a sense of Catullus' fluctuating response to his mistress. For instance, Catullus' lovesick resolve to harden his heart against Lesbia is followed by the poet's admission that even if he cares less, he still loves more; that the flame burns even brighter. Similarly, Catullus' declaration that he could never abuse his beloved is followed by one of his most excoriating – and obscene – attacks on her.[55]

Such changes are in keeping with the teasing spirit of the original poetry and like Catullus' own playful intertextual references to earlier classical literary tradition, they aim to engage in a continuing dialogue with the text – a dialogue which has been taking place

---

[55] Nos.7 & 8 [Catullus 8 & 72]; Nos.19 & 20 [Catullus 104 & 58].

for centuries. After all, both our response to and perception of Catullus' 'book' has always been in a state of flux. To European Renaissance poets, for instance, No.36 [Catullus 16], with its clear division of writer from work, was the quintessential Catullan verse, regardless of the obscenities in its opening and closing lines. More latterly, the Lesbia poems have often garnered most attention, with the lament for Catullus' dead brother a close second.[56] Today, perhaps, with lovers' kisses and quarrels the currency of a myriad popular songs and loose social groupings replacing family ties, Catullus' poems about friendship and social interactions, the ironic, self-mocking tales of social pretension and social embarrassment, move more into focus. For there are and always will be as many Catulluses as there are readers to laugh with him – and scholars to dissect the jokes. As Yeats wrote of his 'old, learned, respectable bald heads':

> Lord, what would they say
> Did their Catullus walk that way?[57]

[56] Imitated, for example, by Tennyson's poem 'Frater Ave atque Vale' from *Tiresias and Other Poems*, 1885.
[57] Yeats, 'The Scholars', in *The Wild Swans at Coole*, 1919.

Dedication to Cornelius Nepos

To whom can I dedicate this little book,
polished, new, just smoothed and buffed by pumice grind?
Cornelius, to you: for you always put
such faith in these poems, these trifles of mine,
even those days when, alone in Italy,
you rolled out three tomes of our world history –
well-researched, by Jupiter, and such hard work.
So take charge of this slight book, for what's it's worth,
for what it might weigh: appointing you patron
should keep it fresh for future generations.

1 *In Love – and Hate – With Lesbia*

I feel it so – and I'm crucified

1: Lesbia's Kisses

Time to live and let love, Lesbia,
count old men's cant, their carping chatter,
cheap talk, not worth one last penny piece.
You see, suns can set, can rise again
but when our brief light begins to wane
night brings on one long unending sleep.
So let me have a thousand kisses,
then a hundred, a thousand *gratis*,
a hundred, a thousand, on increase.
Then, when we've made our first million,
we can cook the books, just smudge the sums
so no evil eye can spy, sully,
by reckoning up our final tally.

2: More Kisses

You ask how much kiss-kissing, Lesbia,
is enough for me, enough and more.
I say: count each grain of Libyan sand
seed-scattered across Cyrene shores,
by steamy shrine of Jove Oracular,
sacred tomb of Battus, stammerer;
or count the many stars at dead of night
that guard men's stolen, secret passions:
for to kiss, to kiss so many kisses
is enough for crazed Catullus – more,
and too many to count for all their spies,
those wagging tongues now cursed with lies.

3: Lesbia's Pet Sparrow

Sparrow, my own sweetheart's sweetness,
whom she teases as she pleases,
puts you on her lap for petting,
gives you fingertips for pecking,
then whips you up to sharper nips –
for when impassioned, burning bright,
she likes to play such games of sleight;
small solace for her lovesickness
until fierce fever seems to rest:
to tease you as she does, just so,
would ease the torture of my soul...

* * * *

...as prized as the golden apple
was, some say, by fleet-footed girl,
loosening her virgin's girdle,
long-tied, long ago, long ago...

4: Death of a Sparrow

Mourn all Loves and mourn all Cupids,
mourn all men who think and feel it:
for my sweetheart's sparrow is dead,
sparrow, my own sweetheart's sweetness,
dearer to her than sight itself –
a honey boy who knew his joy
better than any child mother,
he would never flap from her lap
but hopped hither and tripped thither,
greeted her with cheep and chitter:
today he walks that shady way
from whence (we sense) none may return.
So shame on you, you shameless shades
of Orcus, who take what's precious,
reduce it all to ash and urn:
of precious pet I've been bereft.
Oh woe is you, our poor sparrow,
your mistress weeps – and at your death,
eyes slightly swollen, touched with red.

5: On Seeing Lesbia: A Translation of Sappho

That man to me seems the equal of a god;
that man – dare I say? – surpasses the divine,
the one who sits by you, who time after time
       looks on you, who hears

you as you laugh so sweetly, while I'm in hell,
senses shredded, torn apart; for when I see
you there, Lesbia, there's nothing left of me –
       [no voice to speak of]

as my tongue is numbed, my lips struck dumb; pale fire
trickles down my limbs, my ears resound, ring-ting
with their own thunder, and my eyes are covered
       by these dark nights, twin.

          * * * * *

Leisure is your death, Catullus, your despair:
in leisure you bask, too much of not enough;
for at their leisure kings are lost, such ancient
       cities turned to dust.

6: Keeping Bad Company

Up for It Inn and its uppity inn-mates,
nine down from the sign of Castor and Pollux,
what makes you think you alone have the bollocks,
sole rights to fuck any old girl you fancy
and then call the rest of us goat-like, randy?
Or now that you are lined up like bar-room fools,
a hundred or two, do you think I won't wait
to stuff you in centuplicate, one sitting?
Well, think on: believe me, I will ball you all,
daub your pricks on every spare inch of wall.
For my girl has left me, evades my embrace –
the one loved more than any other could be,
over whom I have fought long wars, and many –
to set up stall there. Now, she's loved by all: great
and good, men of wealth, even – to her disgrace –
weaklings, wastrels, such low-life inferiors;
and above all by you, most hirsute of youths,
rabbit-runt from rabbit-rich Iberia,
Egnatius, of Celtica Cuniculous,
bewhiskered, bearded, oh so suave and refined,
teeth bleached white by your finest Spanish urine.

7: Catullus' Resolve

You wretch, Catullus, just stop this faking
and write off now what is faded, failing.
Once you had dazzling sunshine, your skies glowed,
days you'd go anywhere on her say-so –
the one you loved as no other will be.
There was time for laughter, to joke, to tease,
when you said yes (and she didn't say no);
oh, you had dazzling sunshine, your skies glowed.
Now she demurs so you too must abjure,
don't play the fool or follow her allure,
but see it through, hold on, hold out, harden.
Fare well, girl, Catullus plays the hard man,
won't persist if you resist, beg where shunned –
though you'll regret it when you're begged by none.
You witch, what life now do you think you've earned?
Who will posses you? Whose love will you see?
Who'll obsess you? Whose will you seem to be?
Who will caress you ? Whose lips will you burn?...
Come on now, Catullus, hold up, harden.

8: Catullus (Almost) Stands Firm

You used to say Catullus was your only vice,
Lesbia, that above Jove it was I you cared for;
I said I valued you not like the world his wife
but as a father prizes sons or sons-in-law.
Now I know you, and although the flame burns brighter,
you seem capricious, not so precious, I confess.
How can that be? you ask me. It's simple: hurt a
lover and it might make him love more but care less.

9: Asking Furius and Aurelius For Help

Furius and Aurelius, Catullus' close friends
and fellow travellers, whether he enters
into Indies where waves roar on eastern shores
        as the known world ends

or urbane Urcanes, soft-living Arabians,
the shaggy Sagae, shot-bringing Parthians
or those smooth seas which seven-mouthed Nile befouls,
        discolours, darkens;

whether he makes his advance on the Alps *haute*,
views those testimonials to Caesar's might –
Gallic Rhine, the rough Channel, or the Britons,
        ugly and remote;

and if they're prepared for these, should gods divine
decree, I'd like to ask for one further part:
pass these words on to my girl, not too many
        and not quite so kind:

let her live well and fare well with paramours
she clasps in her embrace three hundred times – more,
loving none, having all, over and over
        just breaking their balls;

say not to lament my love, see then as now,
which, thanks to her, has fallen like a flower
at the far meadow's edge, touched and then devoured
        by the passing plough.

10: Blaming – and Forgiving – Lesbia

It was your fault, Lesbia, my mind was led astray
(although doing the good deed took it half the way);
now I couldn't start to care if you do repent,
wouldn't cease to love even if you don't relent.

11: A Worthless Promise

There's nobody, my woman says, she would rather wed
than me – no, not if Jupiter himself should court her:
so she says, but what a woman says when in your bed
should be written on the wind, in fast-flowing water.

12: The More Loving One

No woman can say she's been loved so much, so long,
as truly Lesbia has been loved in my heart.
No trust or faith could ever be so great, so strong,
as that which lies in this love for you – on my part.

13: A Rival for Lesbia: Ameana

Hail girl, with not the neatest of noses,
nor the smallest of feet, nor eyes that square,
nor slender fingers, a mouth that closes,
and no tongue you could ever call refined:
it's *you* that bankrupt Mamurra's feeling,
the one provincials deem so pleasing?
The height of beauty in Gaul Cisalpine?
The one with whom our Lesbia's compared?
O such times, so foolish, so demeaning!

14: A Rival for Catullus: Lesbia's Brother

Lesbius is sitting pretty: Lesbia loves him best,
far more than you and all your kith and kin, Catullus.
Well, this pretty boy may sell Catullus, and kith and kin –
on condition: find me one bastard friend who'll kiss him.

15: Another Rival for Lesbia: Quintia

They say Quintia's attractive: yes, she's fair, tall,
and stands up straight – each of these good points, I admit.
But 'attractive'? There's no real charm I can recall,
in her whole being not a grain of salty wit.
Lesbia *is* attractive, lovely through and through:
the thief of every woman's charms, their lovers' tools.

16: Another Rival for Catullus: Quintius

Quintius, if you must have Catullus in debt
to his eyes, or anything more precious yet,
don't take this love from him, for it means more, I swear,
than his eyes, or anything more precious far.

17: Fooling Lesbia's Husband

Husband present, Lesbia rails at me, abuses,
which seems to please the poor old fool, greatly amuses.
Ass, what do you know? If she forgot me, was tight-lipped,
she would be cured: yet while she snarls and contradicts,
she not only thinks of me, but, even more germane,
she's angry. That's it: she's inflamed and so she says my name.

18: Fooling Around

Lesbia keeps abusing me, she disagrees
with me: I'm damned if Lesbia doesn't love me.
How do I know? We're playing games and here's the score:
I nag non-stop but I'm damned if I don't love her.

19: Fooling Himself

You think I could ever abuse my love, my life,
the one even dearer to me than both my eyes?
You and your clowns can do your worst, do what you like –
I couldn't, and, if I could, then all love would die.

20: To Caelius: Lesbia Strays Again

My Lesbia, Caelius, that Lesbia –
yes, that Lesbia, Catullus' only one,
whom he loved more than himself, his own, his all,
now she's at the crossroads, on a back-street crawl,
skinning the sons of Rome's greatest scions.

21: Catullus' Torment

I hate you. I love you. *How do I do that?* you might cry.
I don't know yet I feel it so – and I'm crucified.

22: Catullus' Fresh Resolve

If men can gain any pleasure from good deeds past,
the belief that they themselves have been true,
not violated sacred trust but held steadfast,
neither men deceived nor the gods abused,
then you, Catullus, have much to look forward to,
such joys to come from this thankless passion.
For whatever each one of us can say or do,
you have said and done in equal ration.
Now all credit's lost, thrown away on thankless heart.
Why crucify yourself, endure torment?
Why not stand firm, return at last to your own path,
stop being wretched when it isn't meant?
It's hard to lay down long-held love so suddenly –
yes, it's hard but somehow it must be done:
this is your one hope, only chance of victory,
possible or not, this war must be won.
O gods, if you can take pity, if ever you've
bought comfort at our very hour of death,
look on this wretch and if he's lived in rectitude,
tear away this plague, this perniciousness,
the paralysis creeping down through all my limbs,
numbing delight, laying desire to waste.
It's not that I'm asking her to show her feelings,
nor for miracles – that she should be chaste:
I just want to be healed, throw off this foul sickness.
O gods, I've been devout, you grant my wish.

23: A Reconciliation

If good things come to those who wait, who want and wish
but never hope, then here's true comfort for the soul –
yes, Lesbia, comfort dearer to us than gold
now you have been restored to me who's longed for this;
restored to me who longed but did not hope, restored
to me of your own accord – my red-letter day!
What man is luckier than I? Who else can say
they have all in life they've ever wished for – and more?

24: A Love That Lasts Forever

You put it to me, my life, that this love we share,
this delightful love of ours, will last for all time:
Great gods, make sure that she truly means what she swears
and says it sincerely, a heartfelt communion,
so that we may live through the span we are assigned
in an everlasting bond, this holy union.

II *Prostitutes, Pimps and Not So Respectable Women*

Obliging girls...are always prized

25: An Afternoon with Ipsitilla

Please please me, dear Ipsitilla,
my own sweetness, my so clever,
invite me in for siesta
and I'll come – but at your leisure.
Don't block your passage, fold down flaps,
slip off out for other pleasures.
Hold on, get set, let's fill the gap:
nine full-time, full-on, fuck-fuckings;
just say you're game, just say you will,
you see I've eaten, had my fill,
yet still my lunch-box is bulging.

26: Ameana's Delusions

Ameana, the girl who goes and goes,
has the nerve to charge me ten thousand whole –
you know, the girl with the big, beaky nose,
the one that bankrupt Mamurra's feeling.
Call in her next of kin, put her in care,
send out for her friends and physicians;
for the girl is insane, she's not all there:
she needs a brass mirror above the bed
so she can reflect on her own ceiling.

27: Aufillena's Broken Promise

Obliging girls, Aufillena, are always prized,
they do what they say and they reap their reward;
but you've lost my favour: you promised and you lied,
doing wrong by doing nothing untoward.
The honest would do the deed (the chaste won't offer);
you give, my dear girl, to take back, undeterred –
the cheat of a thief, worse than grasping back-street whore
who sells herself in body as well as word.

28: Rapacious Rufa

Rufa, of Bologna, sucks off Rufulus
(though married to Menenius); you'll find her
at graveyards, snatching scraps from funeral pyres,
rolling after loaves as they roll from the fire,
chased, caught – and laid – by some half-shaved cremator.

29: Insatiable Maecilia: To Cinna

When Pompey was consul, Cinna, two men did the deed
with Maecilia: now he's back, he's in again –
as are these two, but for each of them add ten times ten,
a thousand more: adultery breeds potent seed.

30: Bibulous Postumia: A Drinking Song

Fill up our cups with fine old Falernian,
cup-bearer, pour out a far more pungent brew
as Postumia's latest decree dictates –
our tipple-mistress, drunker than vine-drunk grape.
Be off, diluting waters, good wine's ruin,
go and stay with the abstainers and the prudes:
this man's pure Bacchus – and here's percentage proof.

31: A Wild Woman: an acrostic

Birthed by lioness on Libyan mountain,
reared, I fear, by Scylla, with dog-like roar;
obdurate, bitter, mind closed long ago,
numb to my pleas, a heart you can't perturb –
zealous in spite, in savagery yet more.

32: A Cheating (and Pugnacious) Pimp

Two choices, Silo: give back the ten grand I gave you
for services unrendered, and pick your fight;
or you can keep the cash but, please, stop this raging spite –
oh, while you're at it, you can stop the pimping too.

33: Naso's Greatness

You're a great man, Naso, and a great many men
have split your crack: great man, great rear end.

34: A Familiar Tale

Pretty boy with auctioneer, a man who takes the bids:
we think: he's up for sale – and up for it!

III *Loving Juventius*
(and Hating Furius and Aurelius)

you played with me, my honey-boy

35: Juventius' Kisses

If I were asked to kiss your honey eyes,
Juventius, over, over, again,
I would kiss them three hundred thousand times;
for I could never numb my hunger pai,
not if the crop of our kiss-kiss-kisses
was as rich as ripened corn at harvest.

36: Furius and Aurelius' Disapproval

Bugger off and get stuffed, Aurelius
prick-sucker, and dick-lover Furius,
if you keep taking me at my verses –
that if 'sensuous', I'm not quite virtuous.
Goodness in a poet might be fitting,
it's just not essential for his scribblings;
in fact they only can have spice and bite
if they're sensuous – and virtuous? Not quite.
They should stir us, get us roused (not just boys
but men who've lost all movement in the loins).
But you, you read my 'million kisses'
and have me half a man, mawkish, missish.
Still I think you will find me hard enough
as I bugger you both and stuff you up.

37: Juventius' Betrayal

So many, Juventius, to pick and choose from,
one fine man to find, so why pick and woo this one,
who sits and rots in rotten borough Pisaurum,
an out-of-towner peakier than peeling bronze;
to him you give your heart, him you place above me –
the nerve! – and then don't seem to know you've done the deed.

38: Furius' Poverty

Furius, you have neither slave nor cash,
no beds to bug, walls to web, hearths to ash
but you do have father and stepmother
(whose teeth could grind granite to fine powder)
and you and your parent live without strife
along with parent's thin, grin-on-stick wife.
It's no wonder: you health is always rude;
your digestion is good, no fears haunt you,
of fires, collapsing roofs or chimney-pots,
the threat of violent crimes, poison plots –
dangers that befall those with wealth and home.
Yet your bodies are withered to the bone
(or whatever might be more shrivelled, parched)
by sun's heat, winter's cold, fast after fast.
But could things be any better, more blessed?
You don't sweat or salivate in excess,
have foul phlegm, a nose running in green snot.
Cleanliness indeed, but here what's cleaner:
your arse, whiter still than salt in cellar
(for you shit no more than ten times a year
and then it's harder than bean or pebble;
rub it in your hands and watch it crumble,
without even dirtying fingertips).
So please don't spurn your blessings, Furius,
don't devalue or denigrate your lot,
as for a hundred thousand loan from us,
no way: be satisfied with what you've got.

39: Juventius Adds Insult to Injury

Delicate bud of Juventi tree –
of those we know and those that have been,
all those generations still to come –
you can let him have Midas' gold touch,
that man who has neither slave nor cash,
but don't let yourself be loved by him
Is the man not fine? you ask. Oh yes –
a 'fine man' with neither slave nor cash:
put your case, please, for or against us:
but still the man won't have slave or cash.

40: Furius' Security

Furius, your cosy house is secured
against the south breeze and the western gusts,
the fierce north wind and the east – yes, secured
for a cool fifteen thousand, two hundred:
such a dreadful, shiver-inducing draft!

41: Catullus' Agony

You played with me, my honey-boy, so I pilfered
one small kiss as sweet as sweet ambrosia.
And yet, Juventius, it wasn't without cost:
for hours, I recall, I was nailed on the cross;
I made my excuses, so many tears I cried –
nothing, it seemed, could make your anger subside.
For deed done, your soft knuckles wiped away the tears
that wet your lips as if somehow you still feared
lingering infection from my mouth pressed on yours,
like foul, polluting spittle from piss-stained whore.
And you couldn't wait to hand this poor wretch over
to that pest Love, to crucify, to torture;
now my one small kiss was ambrosia no more
but as bitter as bitterest hellebore.
Still, lesson has been learnt by this wretched lover:
I'll never steal again nor kisses pilfer.

42: Hands off Aurelius I

I entrust to you my boy, my darling,
Aurelius, ask this modest favour:
if ever you felt a need or longing
to keep one thing intact, just one thing pure,
preserve this boy for me with modesty.
I don't mean from men at large; I don't fear
those who hurry, scurry, through the streets here,
who pass by, intent on private business,
no, what I fear is you – and your penis,
to good boys, as to bad, it's a danger.
Wave it around as you wish, where you wish,
how you might wish, have it hanging, ready,
with this one, I hope, modest exception.
But if your sick mind, up-for-it frenzy,
compels you, you scum, to commit such sin,
harm a hair on his head with wiles and snares,
you'll suffer for it – believe me, beware:
I will string you up, pack your back passage
with fin-sharp mullets and red-hot radish.

43: Hands off Aurelius II

Aurelius, the Father of all cravings –
not just those past desires that have been and gone
but the hunger we still feel, the lusts to come –
I hear you're longing to bugger my darling.
It's no secret: you seem as one, tease as one,
joined at the hip as you try to try it on.
In vain, my friend: you might lay your little traps
but I'll lay you first with a stiff mouth-stuffing.
If you could get enough I'd hold back, perhaps,
but the fear is you'll teach my boy to gobble,
to gag for it, thirst, like there's no tomorrow.
So put it away, leave modesty untouched
or you'll end up with your end down, that trap stuffed.

IV *Love, Requited*

loving and being loved, of same mind set

44: The Ballad of Septimius and Acme

Septimius sat his love, his Acme,
on his lap: 'Acme,' he told her, 'my dear,
if I don't love you desperately,
now and even more throughout all the years,
as much as most desperate love can own,
then in Libya or sun-scorched India
let me face a green-eyed lion alone.'
So he spoke. And Cupid to show pleasure
on the left (and on the right) sneezed consent.

But Acme, gently bending back her head,
kissed the love-drunk eyes of her own sweet boy
with wine-dark mouth and crimson lips, then said:
'So, my Septimius, my life, my joy,
let's be slaves to Love, by one master owned,
for I have a brighter, more blistering fire
burning through the soft marrow of my bones.'
So she spoke. And Cupid to show pleasure
on the left (and on the right) sneezed consent.

And now they start out with all good omens,
loving and being loved, of same mind set:
for Septimius Acme is the one
he craves, before all Britain, Syria,
in Septimius alone true Acme
takes delight, desire, in equal measure.
Who has ever seen lovers more happy?
Who a love more fortunate, heaven-sent?

V *Good Friends*

in the fire our own…friendship was forged

45: A Dinner Invitation

You will dine well, my dear Fabullus, at mine
in, let's say – and God willing – a few days' time,
if you bring along the best and the biggest
of suppers, plus a pretty girl for afters,
both wine and salt to season all our laughter.
If, as I say, my witty friend, you bring this,
you will dine well: the thing is, your Catullus
has little more than cobwebs to bulge his purse.
In return, you'll find that we serve our love neat –
or any dish more dainty, more exquisite:
for I'll give you the scent of my girl, my sweet,
as anointed by all the Loves and Cupids;
smell it, and you'll bless the day that you were born
so sniff it up, Fabullus, become all horn.

46: A Welcome Return

Veranius, of all my companions
you stand out, my one in a million,
are you back among us, at your own hearth's shrine
with devoted brothers and aged mother?
You are? O this is news to me, happy, dear!
I shall see you safe, hear of Iberia,
of places, races, exploits etcetera,
tales as only you can tell. But leaning in,
drawing you near, I will close those lips with mine,
kiss those laughing eyes. Oh of all happy men
who could be more blessed than I, who happier?

47: Flavius' Secret Love

If she wasn't stupid, charmless,
Flavius, you'd tell Catullus,
you'd not keep your darling from us
yet I'm not sure whom you caress,
this febrile tart you're shamed to own –
for your nights aren't spent alone.
Your bed can't talk but garlands speak
for themselves, that Syrian perfume,
pillows left equally impressed
on both sides, bed-springs that squeak, creak,
somehow creep out across the room.
Don't hide: your sins will find you in.
Why? Your poor crutch looks so fucked out –
proof that you've been fooling about.
So tell all, for better or worse:
let me raise you to the heavens,
you and your love, through my charmed verse.

48: Keeping the Secret: to Cornelius

If secrets are ever passed from trusting friend to trusted –
someone well-known for their abiding loyalty –
then, Cornelius, I'm bound by those laws of privacy,
as silent – sshh! – as the hushing sun god Horus.

49: Caelius (and Quintius) in Love

Caelius and Quintius, two young men of Verona,
are pining for Aufillenus and Aufillena,
one for the brother, the other for the sister, which lends
keeping it in the family a truly sweet new sense.
To which of them should I give my vote? Caelius, it's yours;
for in the fire our own particular friendship was forged,
when passion's maddening flames scorched me to my marrow.
Be happy Caelius: in this love, plough your own furrow.

50: Searching for Camerius I

What we're asking, if, by chance, it's no trouble,
is for you to reveal your shady bolt-hole:
you I've looked for on the Campus Minimus
in all the book shops, the Circus Maximus;
you at the holy temple of Highest Jove
then again in Greatest Pompey's portico.
My friend, I have even accosted street tarts
though they seemed, I must say, innocent enough.
'Hand him over,' I kept insisting, 'you brass-
faced tramps, look, give me back my Camerius.'
'Brass?' said one, as she pulled down her dress, 'try this:
he's gone into hiding in my rosy tits.'
I just can't bear this labour of Hercules;
the aloof way, my friend, you're hiding from me.
So speak up now, tell us where you might be found,
be bold, be brave, share all, publish and be damned:
are you being held in thrall by milk-white girls?
Though if you hold your tongue, if you were to curl
your lips, you'll throw away the fruits of passion –
Venus revels in loose talk, tittle-tattling.
But if it's what you want, I'll let you play dumb
just let me play my part in your liaisons.

51: Searching for Camerius II

...not if I were forged of steel like Cretan Talos,
not if I were Ladas, wing-sandaled Perseus,
not if I were carried by flying Pegasus,
or Rhesus' swifter, snow-white, two-horse chariots;
or anything light-as-feather-footed, flying,
or, I should add, that can also follow the wind;
harness them all, Camerius, on me bestow –
I would still be wearied through to my bone-marrow
eaten out by exhaustion, this great lassitude,
tired of searching high and low, my good friend, for you.

52: Caecilius' Epic Love

Please, papyrus, tell Caecilius
the love poet, my companion,
to come to Verona, leave Novus
Comus and the shores of Larium.
For I have some new cogitations
for him to chew, from his friend and mine.
So, if he's wise, he'll eat up the miles,
even if some fair girl calls him back
a thousand times, more, on his way out,
arms round neck, begging him to unpack.
For if my sources aren't in doubt,
she's wasting away, consumed with love;.
ever since she read his unfinished
opus – 'O mistress of Dindymus' –
the flames have gnawed her to the marrow,
poor little thing. But who can blame her?
For the girl's as well-versed as Sappho
and it starts well, his *Magna Mater*.

53: Writing Poems with Licinius Calvus

Yesterday, Licinius, with time,
we fooled around in my back pages
(for we'd agreed to be salacious):
scribbling down verses, both yours and mine,
playing with rhythm, inflection, stress,
swapping rolls over laughter and wine.
I went home inflamed, Licinius,
by your charm and wit, and so wretched
that I couldn't bring myself to eat
or close my eyes in a second's sleep
but tossed on my bed in frenzy's hold,
longing for the dawn, for night to end,
to speak to you, be with you again.
Afterwards, worn-out with toil, half-dead
on my confining bed, I composed
this poem for you, my teasing friend,
so you, too, could see and feel my pain.
But take care, dear one, don't be too hard,
don't spit them back, these imprecations;
for Nemesis will rewrite my wrongs,
most severe of gods: beware her barb!

54: Calvus' Stature

This made me laugh: in the gallery at court
someone was marvelling as my Calvus talked
(he had Vatinius well and truly banged),
praising his eloquence by a throw of hands:
'God, that little prick can certainly expound!'

VI *Bad Poets*

disease of the age, unreadable poets

55: Calvus' Prank

If I didn't love you, sweet teasing Calvus,
far more than my own eyes, then for today's gift
I'd hate you with the hate of Vatinius;
for what have I said or done to deserve it
that you're killing me now with all these poets?
May the gods frown down on whichever client
settled accounts with this roll of miscreants
(unless, as I suspect, it's that schoolmaster
Sulla, settling his debts by setting these texts,
then I bear no hate, have no complaint to make:
at least your hard work receives due recompense).
God, here's as cursed a verse as one might expect –
a book, I know, you sent to your Catullus
to finish him off, to floor and to bore us
on Saturnalia, our day for pleasure.
No, not so fast, you can't escape, my false friend,
for if this long night of torment ever ends
I'm off to the bookshops to buy Caesius,
Aquinus and Suffenus, all poison pens,
to pay you back in full for your own torture.
Until then, goodbye, farewell, it's time to quit:
let those bad feet limp away, lines and couplets,
disease of the age, unreadable poets.

56: Suffenus' Delusions: to Varus

Suffenus, you know intimately,
Varus, his wit, charm and urbanity
and that he writes a good deal of poems –
say a thousand, perhaps tens of thousands,
copied out, not on our scraps, worn, re-used,
but on Royal Leaf, in brand new volumes,
tied with red ribbon, embossed, so well-tooled,
ruled with lead and by pumice finely smoothed.
But read them: Suffenus, city slicker,
seems far more goat-milker or ditch-digger;
that's how he alters, how perceptions shift.
What to make of it ? One minute a wit,
all that's sharper than sharp, or so it seems,
the next duller than dullest of bumpkins –
at least when he lifts a poem, yet is
never happier than when writing it:
he inspires himself, he admires himself.
Still, we've all had the same failing, all felt
we know or act the Suffenus ourselves:
we all look ahead, know but half the facts –
can't see the baggage that's on our own backs.

57: Recovering from Reading Sestius' Speech

Farm of ours, whether in Sabinum or Tibur,
(those of you who choose to aver the latter
bear Catullus no ill, while those who prefer
to spite him tend to stake all on Sabinum) –
if Sabine or (more precisely) Tiburtine,
how I've enjoyed my sojourn in your out-of-town
manor, getting rid of a nasty cough here,
if not wholly underserved, since my stomach,
sniffing out banquets, was the one who gave it;
eager to be Sestius' guest for dinner,
I devoured his Support-Antius-Now speech,
a poisonous (and pestilence-ridden) piece.
It left me cold – and with this constant coughing
so racking that in your fold I took refuge
to recoup through indolence and nettle soup.
Recovered now, my thanks and praise I proffer
for not taking revenge on my misdoings.
And I won't complain if on reopening
Sestius' foul scribblings, a cough and sniffle
comes not to me but to Sestius himself
who only asks me when he's bad book on shelf.

58: One Good Poet to Three Bad

My friend Cinna's *Smyrna* has been published at last,
after nine autumns and nine winters have passed –
Hortensius, meanwhile, churns out epics in one go...
....
...*Smyrna* will travel to sacred streams in Cyprus,
turn the pages, as Time grows grey, for all ages,
while Volusius' *Annals* shrivel by the Po,
loose wrapping for mackerel, tomorrow's wet fish.
For my friend's short masterpiece is close to my heart;
let the mob take Antimachus' inflated art.

59: Catullus Bad, Cicero Good

Most eloquent of Rome's greatest scions,
all there are, all there have been, Cicero,
all there will be today and tomorrow;
receive these thanks, profuse, acknowledging,
from Catullus, the worst of all poets –
as much the worst poet, I contend here,
as you are our best public defender.

60: Even Bad Poets Have Their Uses

Volusius' *Annals*, shit-smeared sheets,
help me to fulfil my girl's promise:
for by the holy Loves and Cupids
she vowed that if I turned a new leaf,
stop letting loose my fierce iambics,
she'd give the very 'worst of poets' '
most worthless work to limp-footed Lord
of fire, in hapless logs let it roast;
for she thought it such a clever joke,
that worst of girls, to pledge her word.
O Venus, spawned from azure ocean,
enshrined at sacred Idalium
and barren Urium, at Ancon,
reed-rich Cnidus, Amathus, Golgi,
Adriatic Dyrrach, sailors' ease:
sign this vow as paid up, acted on
(if it's not too dry, dispassionate)
For these *can* go into the fire's heat,
blown out with boorishness, so inept,
Volusius' *Annals*, shit-smeared sheets.

61: Battle Lines

Come, hendecasyllables, full division,
all you are, where you are, what you are, come all,
she sees me as a joke, for her derision,
that scabrous tart, who won't hand back our scribblings
so if you can, if I have your permission,
let's surround her, hound her, for restitution.
Who is she? you might ask. Well, here's a vision:
she struts like a slut, laughs like she's in some farce,
has the face of a Gallic dog – and my feet.
Crowd round her now to demand restitution:
'You sad, scrofulous tart, hand back our notebooks;
hand back, sad scrofulous tart, our notebooks now!'
You don't care? You're filth, a whore-house full of tarts
or whatever could be more scabrous than that.
But there's no time to rest, think we've done enough;
if nothing else, we must squeeze a shaming blush
from that brazen, canine, dog-bitch of a face,
so shout it out again, be louder, shameless:
'You sad scrofulous tart, hand back our notebooks;
hand back, sad scrofulous tart, our notebooks now!'
But we're no further forward. She gives no slack.
You need to change the method and the mission
to see if you can make any impression:
'Sweet and modest heart, please hand our notebooks back.'

VII *The Linen Thieves*

when his fellow diners' backs are turned...

62: Asinius' Dinner-party Tricks

Asinius Maruccinus, it's not right
what your left hand's doing: in wine and laughter
you're lifting our napkins when we're not looking.
You think you're clever? You fool, it's impolite,
just about as cheap and graceless as one gets.
You don't believe me? Believe your young brother,
Pollio, who'd pay out to cancel your thefts –
one talent – a boy replete with charm and wit,
urbane, so they say, a true sophisticate.
Hand back my napkin as soon as possible
or expect three hundred hendecasyllables;
I'm not motivated here by loss or gain,
just an *aide-memoire* of my most loyal friend,
a gift of Fabullus – and Veranius –
who sent Saetaban towels direct from Spain;
so you see, it's my duty to prize them best
like dear old Veranius – and Fabullus.

63: Thallus Turns More Tricks

Bum-boy Thallus is soft as bunny's fur,
as goose-down or delicate inner ear
or an old man's drooping, mothballed penis,
yet when his fellow diners' backs are turned
he's more rapacious than some wind-tossed storm –
so send back my best cloak you snatched away,
Saetaban towels, Bithynian inlay,
which you display, you fool, like prized heirlooms;
prise them from your sticky claws, return soon
or you'll be shamed as burning, branding whips
inlay your downy back with my fresh marks
until you toss this way, that, like small ship
stranded, all at sea, caught in these sharp blasts.

64: A Father and Son Team

Our most renowned pair of bath-house thieves –
father Vibennius, rent-boy son
(the former's hand is the stickier,
the latter's arse-hole the greedier) –
should both leave town for nether regions
or for hell; father's many bath-thefts
are well-known and son's hairy buttocks
a no-go, won't fetch a penny piece.

VIII *Not Such Distinguished Features*

who can separate foul from clean?

65: Egnatius' Teeth

Because Egnatius has gleaming white teeth
he beams, come what may. If in court supporting
the accused, as the defence spins tales of woe
he beams; if at a funeral pyre mourning
some only son, as a mother's tears flow,
he beams. Yes, you've guessed, whatever, whenever,
wheresoever, he beams. It's like a disease
with him, not nice and certainly not civil.
So a word of warning, good Egnatius,
if you were civilised – Sabine, Tiburtine,
or some pinched Umbrian, podgy Etruscan,
or a brown-skinned, buck-toothed Lanuvine,
or Transpadane (to name my land, if I can),
or whoever cleans their teeth the good old way,
I still wouldn't want you to beam, come what may;
for nothing's more absurd than an absurd grin.
But in Iberia – and you're Iberian –
whatever water gets passed in the morning
is used to bleach the teeth, redden round the rims:
so the yet more dazzling your foolish smile is,
the more we know you'll have drunk of your own piss.

66: Arrius' Haitches

We say 'advantages', he says 'hadvantages',
we say 'artifice,' Arrius has 'hartifice';
in fact, he hammers it out to his heart's content –
such are his haspirations to heloquence.
His mother and uncle, I hear, once did the same;
maternal grandparents must have share of blame.
But now he's been posted East and our ears are eased;
hear those hated words, as smooth, soft, as we please
until they lose their horror, don't seem so harmful.
And then, a message comes, hideous, hawful:
since Arrius crossed the sea we call 'Ionian'
the whole world, it seems, now says 'Hionian'.

67: The Curse of Rufus' Armpits

Have you ever wondered, Rufus, why no woman you know
wants to slide under you, let you crush her slight bones?
Not if you enticed her, delighted her, with fine-weave clothes
or the pleasures of sparkling, semi-precious stones?
For an evil rumour here costs you dear: that you've released
a fierce goat, let it live in your hollowed armpits.
They're all afraid of it – and no wonder: for it's a beast
of bad odour, a lover no girl would admit.
So either slaughter that known nose-nuisance now, do it in
or stop wondering why they all keep on running.

68: Rufus' Contagion Starts to Spread

I hear that goat-arm syndrome is getting in the way
and those gout-feet too are rightly stopping play;
for the man who's been putting your love through her paces
has been tainted, infected by your traces.
Now when they both fuck, they are tormented both the same:
she suffers by smelling, he by huge swelling.

69: Aemilius' Mouth (and Arse)

I thought, so help me God, that I couldn't tell
if Aemilius' mouth or arse made that smell;
for mouth, arse, who can separate foul from clean –
but on balance, yes, the arse is less obscene
since it lacks teeth. His mouth's are sesquipedal,
poking out of gapped gums, spokes on rotted wheel,
besides, it grins like a cunt, split, fissured
like a mule pissing at the height of summer.
Still he fucks them all, seems irresistible
(for which he should do donkey-work on treadmill).
As for the women, let's try to define them:
they would lick the arse of diarrhoed hangman.

70: Victius' Tongue

Victius, you, if anyone, we call foul-mouthed
(ditto gossips, gassers, those who give scandal);
for with that tongue, if occasion ever allows,
you could lick arseholes, swineherds' shit-soiled sandals.
If you want to kill us anywhichway, Victius,
open wide: anywhichway you'll get your wish.

71: Gellius' Lips I

I can't explain it, Gellius, I just don't know
how in morning light, or after siesta –
the quiet naps we snatch on long days of summer –
those rose-red lips seem smattered with hoar-white snow.
We need clues: dare we believe the word on the street
that you dine in on prime hunks of mid-cut meat?
It is true: poor Victor's shattered balls confirm it,
their mouth-milked seed spattered across your pale lips.

72: Gellius' Lips II

...And now more shame in this: that your repulsive spit
defiles, pisses, on a pure young girls' lips.
You won't get away with it: time will know your feats –
who you are: let old woman Gossip speak.

IX *Incest Isn't Best*

is this the sort of sin you now have in sight?

73: Aufillena's Adultery

To live in bliss, Aufillena, one man for life,
is praise brides prize as the highest pinnacle.
But much better to sleep with anyone you like
than to mother cousins by your own uncle.

74: Uncle Gallus' Family Ties

Gallus is a family man; he has two brothers,
one with charming wife, charming son for other.
Gallus is a nice man: he sees a sweet liaison,
arranges for nice wife to sleep with nice son.
Gallus is a stupid man: he forgets he's married too:
an uncle who proves how uncles can be fooled.

75: Gellius' Uncle (and Aunt)

All uncles like to lecture, Gellius heard,
to tut-tut those who enjoy a tumble.
And so to knock the knockers, he then knocked off
uncle's wife – which rather silenced uncle.
Now he does as he likes: if he were to fuck
uncle's mouth, uncle couldn't say a word.

76: Gellius' Other Relations

What does it mean, Gellius, this mother, sister itch,
up all night, clothes strewn, all three without a stitch?
And what is this, denying uncle marital rights –
is this the sort of sin you now have in sight?
Such sins, Gellius, that not even the far Ocean
nor his remote wife and daughters, could cleanse them;
for there's no greater crime, no worse could ever follow
if you bent your head, opened legs, and swallowed.

77: More of Gellius' Relations

Gellius has lost weight. And why not? With a mother
so lively – and sporting – such a charming sister,
so decent an uncle, girls in so many places,
all related, why not look emaciated?
So what if he'll only touch those who are forbidden –
he still has more than enough there to keep him thin.

78: Gellius' Offspring

May a Magus be begat from this profane conjunction
of Gellius and Mum, steeped in divination
(for it best behoves the Magi to be born a son's son –
if there's an ounce of truth in Persian religion);
so let their son venerate his gods with pleasing refrain,
separate grease from grist on sacrifical flames.

79: Catullus' Relations with Gellius

The reason, Gellius, I'd hoped you would be loyal
in this wretched, this desperate love of ours
was not because I'd come to know you, thought you steadfast,
could keep your straying thoughts from shame or scandal:
but because she was neither mother, sister, to you
the woman whose love gnaws me to the marrow;
and if our relations have been too close, too narrow –
they didn't seem close enough to interest you.
But you disagreed. For such is the pleasure you take
in all crimes, the wrong-doing you love to make.

X *In Mourning*

hail and farewell

80: To Calvus in Time of Grief

If any welcome word can reach the wordless tomb,
any crumb of comfort come from our grief, Calvus –
the way we might yearn for old loves to be renewed,
weep for friendships that long since slipped away from us –
then Quintilia, you can be sure, will grieve less
at her young death than rejoice at your steadfastness.

81: A Brother's Death

Many the seas, many the lands I have travelled through
and now I come, brother, to these sad rites for you,
that I may perform the final, formal dues of death,
to your silent ashes make my futile address.
For Fate has stolen you from me, robbed me of your self –
alas, my poor brother, a theft unjustly dealt;
so receive these now as parental custom desires,
handed down as our sad due at funeral pyre,
offerings imbued with a brother's many, many tears:
hail and farewell, brother, for all time, all the years.

82: A Letter to Hortalus

Though worn down, Hortalus, by this unrelenting grief,
torn away by cares from the Muses' strict pursuits,
unable, even in mind's eye, to bear their sweet fruit,
tossing, turned, on a wave of pain without relief
(for recently the rising tide of Lethe's waters
has washed the ghost-pale soles of my passing brother –
oh my brother, snatched from my eyes by death's robber stealth
weighted down by Trojan soil, on Hellespont shore,
[will I ever hear your voice or speak to you once more,]
see you, brother, dearer to me than life itself? –
it's true, as I love you now, I'll love you tomorrow,
always compose these songs soaked in your death's sorrow,
songs the nightingale sings in shadowed thicket branches,
Procne lamenting the death of her son Itys),
and yet, Hortalus, in the midst of such great sadness,
I send you this translation of Callimachus
lest you think your request in vain, swept off by the wind,
flowing out then in, slipping through my shifting mind,
like an apple sliding off a pure young virgin's lap,
a token sent in secret from her own betrothed,
hidden, forgotten, poor girl, beneath her flowing clothes
but at her mother's step, she leaps up, lets it drop,
sends it tumbling, sets it bumping, out across the ground,
blush stealing across her grave face at being found.

83: A Reply to Manlius' Request for Love Poems

The fact you've sent me this letter, written in your tears,
now you've been bowed down by fortune's bitter blows,
shipwrecked, pitched by foaming waves, to be cast up here,
begging to be saved from death's very threshold –
for sacred Venus allows you neither rest nor sleep,
has left you alone and chaste in unshared bed,
and Muses can't soothe with poems old and sweet
when your troubled mind won't let you rest your head –
yes, it's gratifying that you think me such a friend
ask me for verse, the gifts of Muses, Venus,
but if I feel the duty owed, still I might offend,
for you don't yet know my troubles, Manlius;
I also have been drowning in fortune's high flood water
so don't expect the gifts happiness can bring.
It's true that since I came of age, put on man's toga –
the days youth bloomed with all the delights of spring –
I've had my share of Love's games: nor was she a stranger
to me, bittersweet goddess of joy and pain
but grief at a brother's death robbed me of all pleasure;
my poor brother taken from me to death's gain,
for brother, at your passing, laughter, faith, were fractured,
with you, house, family, line, lie buried as one,
all our pleasures are lost in you, all joys are shattered –
the joys in life your sweet love brought to blossom.
Now even these are driven from my heart, such my loss,
pursuits of the mind, pleasures of the body.
And so, when you write to me 'it's a shame Catullus
stays in Verona, where men live so poorly,
where even the well-off warm blue bodies in cold beds,'
I see no 'shame', Manlius, just misfortune.
So forgive me if I don't send the gifts you request,
it's because I can't give what grief has taken.
Besides, I have neither books nor library here with me –
I live at Rome, there I have my house, my home,
the place where I'll see out my time, days I might be owed
(here I've dragged just one book-box out of many).

Nevertheless, please, don't take my reticence amiss
or think me somehow mean or ungenerous
when I don't provide your poems, love or otherwise –
I'd gladly have sent both, if there were supplies.

XI *Home and Away*

to rest my head in that longed-for bed

84: A Tale of Old Verona

Colonial town, how you wish
      for fun and games on your bridge;
You're ready and willing to dance
      but fear those second-hand planks
on your poor crossing, trembling legs
      which shake, quake, beneath your tread
as if it might fall flat on back
      sink in the mire on impact:
so let's have a new bridge here please
      to satisfy all your needs.
one to withstand priests' prancing rites
      on Leaping Leg-Over nights,
then, Colony, on my behalf
      grant the last, the longest laugh.
There's a certain of my townsmen
      I thought you might throw headlong
from creaking bridge down into mud
      head over heels in the sludge
just there, where your smooth lake becomes
      a dank swamp of boggy scum
as the slime takes a greyish hue
      and the quagmire engulfs you.
For the man's a bore, a nuisance
      hasn't even half the sense
of a toddler, asleep and calmed
      in his father's rocking arms.
His wife is a girl so tender
      a bud on the brink of flower
a girl even more capricious
      than goat-kid, sweet and skittish
someone to nurture at all times
      like grapes ripening on their vines
but she takes fun where she finds it
      – and he doesn't give a fig
no, he can't get aroused by her
      lies as still as felled alder
ham-strung by Ligurian axe
      hewn from tree to wood to ash

he feels it all yet feels nothing
      no deep stirring in the limbs
this fool of a man I mention
      seems blind, deaf and somehow numb
to who he is, if he exists
      and ignorance isn't bliss.
So come on now, make him feel this:
      toss him headlong from your bridge
see if a swift loss of balance
      cures his dull indifference
if his soggy and spineless bent
      stiffens, sticks, in sediment;
like a foot-print or steel horseshoe
      left in claggy mire by mule.

85: A Door-step Gossip in Verona

CATULLUS:
You're a comfort to husbands, good door, and to parents,
so greetings to you, Jove grant you health and wealth,
for they say you guarded Balbus with all due caution,
the days the old man could call this house his home
yet to his son, I hear, you were much more negligent
(when old boy pegged out, son's wife took residence);
so if, as they say, you've swung a different way, tell us,
why did you forsake your former faithfulness?

DOOR:
Look (Caecilius willing, for his house I now frame),
whatever they say, I'm really not to blame,
let them all talk: I'm not the one who's guilty of sin –
believe me, though, with those gossips who can win?
If anything happens, something's stolen, dinner's spoilt,
inside they cry as one: 'Door, it's all your fault!'

CATULLUS:
Still, it's not enough to rely on mere divulgence,
you need to produce proof, hard fact, evidence.

DOOR:
How can I? Nobody asks; they don't want to find out.

CATULLUS:
I do. So tell me, please, dispel all my doubts.

DOOR:
Well, the wife came, divorced, but still virgin, they told me –
some virgin! For she'd been touched up already,
not by first husband whose prick was saggy as sugar
beet, couldn't raise itself to touch his toga,
but former father-in-law, who defiled his son's bed,
spotted, stained, that unlucky house, so it's said,
whether his fell heart was fired by blinding flash of love
or a son far too feeble to do the job,
sterile, seedless, in need of added sinew, stiffness,
something that could get inside a virgin's dress.

CATULLUS:

What a wonderful parent, all devotion on tap,
ready and willing to piss in own son's lap!

DOOR:

But there's more – whispers, particulars, from Brixia,
the city that lies beneath Cycnus' tower
where golden river Mella flows by with gentle stream,
mother-city of Verona, of my dreams,
which cite one Cornelius, a Postumus affair,
of adultery, all kinds of goings-on there.

CATULLUS:

But what if we say: 'You're just a door, how can you know,
you never so much as leave your own threshold?
How can you hear what people say, stuck on a lintel,
an open and shut case, you're not pivotal.'

DOOR:

But often I heard her hushed tones, the tittle-tattle
alone with maids, telling them all the scandals,
naming names, saying what I just said, cited *supra*,
as if she thought I had neither tongue nor ear.
Then she added one more name, which I'll decline to now,
in case he raises his fiery ginger eyebrows;
a tall man, famously sued for false paternity –
you know, the case of the missing pregnancy.

86: Catullus' Yacht

That ship you see there, good friends and guests,
could tell a tale – the swiftest of crafts,
which no keel, she says, could ever pass,
whether oar-palms dipped to help her crest
or sail unfurled: fierce Adriatic
can confirm it, islands Cycladic,
renowned Rhodes and wind-tossed Thracian
Propontis, the rough gulf of Pontus
where ship-to-be was once green forest,
trees with leafy tresses, and mountain
gusts gasped, rippled, through her sighing locks;
Amastris, Cytorus, thick with box,
to you, she claims, this is, has been known –
here she stood tall, trailed palms in waters
and from your heights she bore her master
through narrow straits, safely led him home
whether starboard breezes swept her left,
right, or some fresh tail-wind, Jove-sent, kept
both sheets billowing, boat tacking straight;
for she had no need of vows or prayers
to gods of safe return, as she steered
one last sea to reach this limpid lake.
But that was then: now she navigates
old age's calms, dedicates herself
in peace at last to sailors' guardians –
to twinned Castor and Pollux the twin.

87: Home, At Last, From Bithynia

Of pseud-islands and true islands, Sirmio,
you're the best sight for these eyes, whether Neptune
serves up sea or shore, clear lakes or ocean floor,
how pleased, how relieved I am to call on you,
back – at long last! – from the plains of Thynia
and Bithynians to see you safe once more.
And oh what bliss to dismiss my grief, let go
my weary load, to come home to my own soil,
exhausted by my travel, to rest my head
in that longed-for bed – one spoil worth all the toil.
So greetings, good Sirmio, here's the briefing:
wave now for joy, your laughter for your master's;
and don't be coy, Gardian lake, please please him:
roar with all your force, feel it in your waters.

XII *The Rewards of Office*

travelling light, backs unpacked

88: Never As Much As We Might Say...

Varus dragged me from the forum
to visit his love – I had time –
a two-bit-tart, or so I find,
if not without some style or charm.
When we got there, we talked of this
and that, the present state of play
in Bithynia, how things weighed,
if I'd made much of a profit.
I told them: with none for locals,
governors, or loyal staffers,
who the hell could get palms oiled –
not with that mouth-fucker praetor
whose finger won't lift for his aides?
'But surely,' they say, 'you acquired
something of the best local ware
like, say, litter-bearers?' So I,
to make the girl think me greater,
say: 'True, things weren't so straitened,
my province wasn't so austere,
I couldn't secure eight strong men.'
(In fact I had none, neither here
nor there, who wouldn't buckle
under cracked leg of aged truckle.)
At this, just like some brazen slut,
the girl said: 'My dear Catullus,
could I borrow them for a bit?
I'd love a lift to Serapis.'
'Ah. When I said that I had them,
I forgot – of course – my good friend –
Cinna, that is, Caius – they're his.
Though, in truth, whether his or mine,
I use them as much, all the time...
(But you, you're a bore, a nuisance,
not to allow me this pretence.)'

89: ...Or We Might Hope

Empty-headed Piso's empty-handed staff,
travelling light, backs unpacked – Veranius,
the best of men and you, my Fabullus,
how are things going? Have you both had enough
of frost and famine with that foul glass-rim scum?
Do your accounts show a higher turnover
of debts, as mine did when I served my praetor,
chalking up double entries – of my expense:
Memmius, long, good and hard with that huge shaft
you fucked me up, slowly, as I lay at length.
But the way I see it, as a rule of thumb,
we're all in deep. For no less renowned a prick
has stuffed you both. *Forge favourable friendships?*
No, I say curse them all, gods and goddesses,
shame of our founding fathers, this city's dregs.

90: The Grass Is Always Greener

Porcius and scrawn Socration,
that puffed-up prick Piso's theft-hand men,
the plague and privation of this world,
you're preferred to my Veranius
and Fabullus? For you have lavish
all-day banquets, while my friends languish
on back street-corners, invites on hold.

91: To Pompey and Julius Caesar:
In Protest at Mamurra's Greed

Could anyone see, could anyone bear this,
unless brazen, grasping, prepared to risk it?
For what those long-haired Gauls once had, Mamurra
has now, the spoils of remote Britannia.
Chief bum-boy Pompey, can you see and bear this
as that wretch, all impudence, all imprudence,
flits and flutters around every marriage-bed
like one of Venus' love-birds or Adonis?
Chief bum-boy Caesar, you see this, you bear this?
You are brazen, grasping, prepared to risk it.
Was this the real reason, oh peerless legate,
you've been in that remote, far western island –
so that fucked-out Prick, your tool, can gobble through
two hundred or is it three hundred thousand?
Surely this must be munificence gone mad?
Hasn't that Prick reached his peak, enjoyed enough?
First he squandered paternal inheritance
then Pontus' booty, then (as we're counting up)
Spain's fresh loot – its gold-filled rivers know the rest.
And now he's eying up Gaul, remote Britain?
So why the hell do you both still favour him;
he'll consume it all, every last bit of fat.
Is this the reason, our city's holiest,
father and son-in-law, you've laid all to waste?

92: Mamurra the Prick

Prick's estate at Firmum evidently makes him rich;
of every good blessing he can take his pick:
all kinds of fowl, fish, pastures, meadows, beasts of the field.
But it's no good; for his expenses exceed yield.
I say let him be rich if it means he's left without –
hurrah for fertile fields which make him stony-broke.

93: More Prick

Prick, we hear, can count twenty acres of pasture
and thirty or so of plough. The rest is morass.
So why doesn't he possess the wealth of Croesus,
after all, his estate's as good as you could wish for:
meadows and corn-fields, great forests, vast marsh-lands, ditch,
right up to Hyperborea, northern Ocean?
Yes, every good thing, although he's the best of them –
not the biggest man but by far the biggest prick.

94: Yet More Prick

Prick writes a book, for he wants to mount Olympus;
the Muses toss him off with their prick-sharp pitch-forks.

* * * * *

Prick is priapic. A priapic prick? No surprise.
As they say: boil a pot and the scum will rise.

95: Caesar and Mamurra

They go well together, those shameless bum-boys,
Mamurra and his Caesar, his catamite.
It's no wonder: both are tarred with the same brush,
one by the city and one by Formiae,
polluted, pot-marked, by stains that just won't wash:
sharing their sick lust, twins divided at birth,
well-schooled in the same bed-room and all its joys
(in adulterous sex we've no greater experts),
friends, rivals, for all the little girls they like –
they go well together, those shameless bum-boys.

96: Shunning Caesar

I don't want to please you, Caesar, give you support –
nor need to know what sort of man I don't endorse.

97: Annoying Caesar

There's Otho with his oh so tiny knob-head,
that bumpkin Hirrus and his mud-caked legs,
Libo whose farts are by far his best feature:
come on now, some of these, at least, must rile you –
Sufficius, that warmed-up coffin-dodger?
Still, you'll be angered again by my verses,
oh peerless legate, though they don't deserve it.

98: Catullus in Despair

What's wrong with you, Catullus? Why delay dying?
That carbuncle Nonius squats in curule's chair;
Vatinius seeks public office, falsely swears.
What wrong with you Catullus? Why delay dying?

XIII *The Wages of Sin: Betrayals and Recriminations*

I can hurt you too, exact revenge

99: Love's Punishment: A Joke for Cato

It's so absurd, Cato, you'll have to laugh,
fit for your ears and for all your guffaws;
yes, it's so absurd, you will laugh too much –
as much as you love Catullus, Cato:
you see, I caught some young girl's young fellow
beating his rod. And so, by Love's own law,
I banged him to rights with my own stiff shaft.

100: Cominius the Informer Gets His Just Desserts

Cominius, your hair's white so people decide
it's more than high time this dirty old man died.
First bit to go, public enemy number one,
torn out by greedy vulture, that guilty tongue;
next, eyes to be pecked out by black-throated raven,
dogs to guzzle the guts, wolves wolf what remains.

101: Alfenus' Betrayal

Capricious Alfenus, faithless, duplicitous,
does it feel pity, that hard heart, for your sweet friend?
So you've betrayed me, can't wait to waylay, deceive –
do gods smile on malicious deeds, mendacious men?
Or do you neglect them as you've left this poor wretch?
Tell me: what can men do, where can we place our trust,
for you begged me, you cheat, to surrender my soul,
drew it to you, kept it safe, something precious won.
Now you draw away, and all you've said, all you've done,
is long gone, words in the wind, clouds the sky lets go.
But if you forget, the gods, good faith, remember,
will make you repent, at length, for all harm rendered.

102: Why Expect Any Different?

Stop wanting, stop expecting praise or gratitude,
stop thinking that anyone can become true.
They are all ungrateful: there's no point in kindness –
it wears one out, hinders all that might be best,
or so I find: for nobody is more severe
than the one, the only man, who holds you dear.

103: Rufus' Poison

Rufus, in vain I thought you my friend, for nothing
(nothing? it cost me dear in pain and suffering).
Is this how you've crept up on me, gnawed at my bones,
stripped away all that's good, all that feeds the soul?
Stripped away my life, damn you, like rust, poison,
destroyer, damn you, damn you, of friendship's bond.

104: Cornificius' Defection

Catullus has it bad, Cornificius,
it's bad, by Hercules, and laborious,
yes, worse and worse, by the day and by the hour.
Yet have you done what's obvious, easiest,
offered me consolation, any succour?
I'm angry with you. So that's how my love is?
A little consolation, if you please, here,
something sadder than Simonides' dirges.

105: Ravidus' Insanity

Are you mad, Ravidus, as well as wretched
as you dive headlong into my iambics?
Which god did you bother without all due form
who drives you to stir up this half-wit brawl?
Or do you want to gain fame by any means?
You will do. You're longing to love my darling
but my satisfaction will be longest: this.

Endpiece: A Warning to Gellius

For some time my restless mind has been hunting down
the right words for my versions of Callimachus,
a way to change your closed mind, thwart all your attempts
to hurl hostile missiles at my head, Gellius;
now I see my efforts were in vain, all hopes reversed,
that prayers were futile, pleas too weak to withstand.
Now I'm not just dodging darts, I'm on the offence;
for I can hurt you too, exact revenge – in verse.

APPENDICES

NOTES

Dedication to Cornelius Nepos:
smoothed and buffed by pumice grind: pumice stone was used to smooth the ends of a papyrus roll.

three tomes of our world history: Nepos' now-lost *Chronica* or *History* was published in three volumes.

I *In Love – and Hate – with Lesbia*
For the issues surrounding the 'Lesbia' poems and her identification as Clodia Metelli, see Introduction pp.15-16.

2: More Kisses
kiss-kissing: Catullus apparently invents the word *basiationes* from *basia* ('kisses'), coining a 'learned-sounding polysyllable' (Quinn, 1996: 112).

Cyrene shores: the Latin uses the plural *Cyrenis*, referring to the region of Cyrenaica, as well as to the city itself.

shrine of Jove Oracular: The Libyan temple of the Egyptian god Ammon, associated with Jupiter or Jove by the Romans, contained a renowned oracle.

Battus, stammerer: Herodotus tell the story of how Battus, the legendary founder of Cyrene, consulted the Delphic Oracle about a speech impediment, receiving the reply that he should go to Libya (*The Histories*, 4.154-7). Callimachus, the Hellenistic poet whose work greatly influenced Catullus, came from Cyrene and claimed descent from the hero; in No.82 and 'Endpiece', Catullus refers to Callimachus as *Battiadae*.

3: Lesbia's Pet Sparrow
sparrow: a debate has been raging for centuries over whether Catullus' two sparrow poems contain an obscene double meaning, with the sparrow (Latin *passer*) representing the poet's phallus. Most scholars now reject the theory but it's still good fun.

prized...golden apple...fleet-footed girl: the coda to the poem presents many textual difficulties; as early as the Renaissance, some editors were arguing that it represented a separate fragment and did not belong here. The simile refers to the legend of Atalanta, who agreed to marry whichever of her suitors could outrun her. Hippomenes won by distracting her with a golden apple.

4: Death of a Sparrow
Loves...and Cupids: Veneres Cupidinesque is an expression peculiar to Catullus 'embracing all the agencies and personifications of Charm and Desire' (Goold, 2001: 236).

honey-boy: honey had erotic overtones in classical literature; Catullus' beloved Juventius is also likened to honey in Nos.35 & 41.

5: On Seeing Lesbia: A Translation of Sappho
Translation of Sappho: of Sappho fragment 31 (see Balmer, 1992: 38).

Leisure...: as in No.3 above, it is not clear whether this coda belongs here or not. It certainly does not seem to bear much resemblance to Sappho's version (although, by coincidence, her poem also trails off with a disputed final stanza). Some believe it is from a separate poem while others argue that Catullus might have added it at a later date after his affair with Lesbia was over. No one, though, is certain; as Kenneth Quinn puts it 'I have found myself changing sides so often that I now feel despondent' (1996: 245).

6: Keeping Bad Company

Up for It Inn: in Latin the inn is described as a *salax taberna*, from the verb *salire* 'to leap over', a verb also used of male animal mounting (Adams, 2002: 206).

nine down from the sign of Castor and Pollux: a reference to the temple of the twins Castor and Pollux, which was sited in the south-eastern end of the Forum, alongside, it appears, many taverns.

stuff you: the Latin verb *irrumare* ('to mouth fuck', or force a partner to perform fellatio) does not have an English equivalent. However, it is a common threat in Catullus' verse; inflicting any active sexual act on a passive partner, whether willing or unwilling, was considered humiliating (see No.36 and Introduction p.17).

Celtica Cuniculous: Celtiberia, a district of central Spain, was known for its long-haired rabbits.

hirsute...bewhiskered, bearded: long hair was considered dandyish, although thick beards were worn more by the older, senatorial class – does Egnatius have pretensions to social climbing?

Spanish urine: other sources, such as Diodorus (5.33.5) and Strabo (3.164) also note that the Celtiberians did indeed whiten their teeth in this manner.

9: Asking Furious and Aurelius for Help

Like No.5, written in Sapphics. For a further discussion on the poem see Introduction p.20.

Furius and Aurelius: the pair more usually appear as objects of ridicule and Catullus' rivals (see Nos.36, 38, 40-43). The poet's depiction of them as friends here is probably ironic.

Parthians: the much-feared tribesmen had defeated the Romans in battle in 53 BC.

Nile: in 55 BC, the Romans had helped restore Ptolemy Auletes to his throne.

Caesar...Channel...Britons: the line dates the poem to after Caesar's conquest of Britain in 55 BC. It is also Catullus' only friendly mention of Julius Caesar who is elsewhere savagely lampooned (see Nos.91, 95, 96-97).

breaking their balls: the Latin verb *rumpere*, 'to burst', has an idiomatic use similar to ours in English (see also on No.71).

like a flower...: the simile echoes a Sappho fragment (105c LP, see Balmer, 1992: 58) in which a girl's lost virginity is compared to a hyacinth trampled underfoot by shepherds, in keeping with Catullus' choice of Sapphics as a poetic form here. See Introduction p.20.

10: Blaming – and Forgiving – Lesbia

doing the good deed: the Latin *officium* or 'sense of duty' also had sexual connotations (see Wiseman, 1985: 12).

12: The More Loving One

trust or faith: here, as elsewhere, Catullus uses the language of legal, political and social obligation in an emotional context.

13: A Rival for Lesbia: Ameana

no tongue you could ever call refined: opinion is divided on why not: is it the things she says? Or is it, as Godwin suggests (1999: 162), the things she does with it?

that bankrupt Mamurra: the Latin says only 'the bankrupt from Formiae', identified as Mamurra, an associate of Caesar. Although Catullus berates Mamurra for his acquisitiveness in No.91, he elsewhere ridicules him for squandering his wealth as quickly as he acquired it (see Nos.92-93). He appears again as Ameana's lover in No.26.

14: A Rival for Catullus: Lesbia's Brother

Lesbius...pretty: the Latin *pulcher* or 'pretty' seems to be a pun on the Roman name 'Pulcher', advancing the theory that Lesbia was Clodia Metelli, the sister of Publius Clodius Pulcher, accused of incest with all three of his sisters. Cicero also uses the same 'pretty-boy' pun of Clodius (see *Caelius,* 36).

sell: i.e. into slavery

bastard friend: the Latin puns on *notus* 'well-known' and *nothus* 'illegitimate'.

15: Another Rival for Lesbia: Quintia

salty wit: Latin *sal,* or 'salt', is used, as in English, of both table salt and of risqué talk. See also No.45.

lovers' tools: the Latin *veneres* means 'desires' or 'charms' (see note on No.4), although the single form *venus,* from which the goddess Venus acquired her name, could also be used of a penis (Adams, 2002: 57). Is Catullus' use of the word here a sly dig at Lesbia's infidelities?

16: Another Rival for Catullus: Quintius

Quintius: possibly Quintia's brother, he also appears as the joint suitor, with Caelius, of a pair of siblings in No.49.

17: Fooling Lesbia's Husband

Husband present: commentators see this as further proof that 'Lesbia' is the married (and adulterous) Clodia. Godwin, through, argues that the figure of the cuckolded husband is a stock comic character (1999: 198).

she's inflamed: the idea of love as fire comes from Sappho fragment 31 (see No.5).

19: Fooling Himself

your clowns: the Latin *Tappone* is mysterious. Tappo was a real Roman name but also a stock character in farce, with a possible meaning here of 'clown'. This suits the vagueness of the epigram with no named addressee, although often grouped with the Lesbia poems (see Godwin, 1999: 215).

20: To Caelius: Lesbia Strays Again

Caelius: more ammunition for the theory that 'Lesbia' is Clodia, who was known to have had an affair with M. Caelius Rufus after her husband's death in 59 BC. See Introduction p.15.

skinning the sons: the Latin verb *glubere* literally means 'to peel' but might also have been used in a sexual sense, as in 'retracting the foreskin by intercourse or masturbation' (Adams, 2002: 74). Another suggested inference is the taking of money by false pretences as in English idiom 'to skin' or 'to fleece' (Godwin, 1999: 180).

22: Catullus' Fresh Resolve

Why crucify yourself: the same verb, *excruciare*, as in No.21. The idea of a lover crucified by love also appears in No.41, this time of Juventius' betrayals.

23: A Reconciliation

red-letter day: the Latin reads 'day with a whiter mark', a metaphor derived from the white pebbles ancient Cretan archers dropped in their quivers to mark a happy day.

II *Prostitutes, Pimps and Not So Respectable Women*

25: An Afternoon with Ipsitilla

Please please me: the Latin *amabo* literally means 'I shall love', used colloquially for 'please', a suitable opening for the poem's plea to Ipsitilla.

Ipsitilla: the name has caused much discussion among scholars: is it a diminutive of *ipsa*, 'herself', a colloquial expression among slaves for 'the mistress' (rather like the Irish colloquial 'himself')? The lady in question was probably a high class call-girl, if here a woman of the day rather than of the night.

block your passage: The Latin puns on the similar verbs *obserare*, 'to obstruct' or 'to bolt', and *obserere*, 'to sow'. The English echoes Max Miller's apparently apocryphal joke about meeting a blonde on a high, narrow bridge, supposed to have caused his ban from BBC Radio: 'I didn't know whether to block her passage or toss myself off.'

fold down flaps: the 'flaps' were the leaves of a Roman double-door, although, again, Catullus' purpose here is almost certainly innuendo.

fuck-fuckings: Catullus coins the comic polysyllable *fututiones* from the verb *futuere*, the Latin F-word. (see note on *basiationes*, No.2).

lunch-box is bulging: Catullus puns on *pransus*, a military metaphor which originally meant 'having breakfasted' but came to mean 'ready for action.'

26: Ameana's Delusions

Ameana: Lesbia's big-nosed rival from No.13 returns.

ten thousand whole: according to Cicero, ten thousand *sesterces* was about a year's rent in Rome (*Caelius*, 17).

bankrupt Mamurra: see note on No.13.

her own ceiling: the Latin puns on *aes*, which literally means 'bronze' but was used of both 'money' and 'a mirror'.

27: Aufillena's Broken Promise

Aufillena: seemingly from a respectable family of Verona, she also appears in No.49 and No.73.

doing wrong by doing nothing untoward: the poem is almost the inverse of Max Miller's ditty: 'I like the girls who do/I like the girls who don't. / I hate the girl who says she will / And then she says she won't. / But the girl I love the best of all, / And I'm sure you will say I'm right / Is the girl who says she never does, / But looks as though she might.'

28: Rapacious Rufa

scraps from funeral pyres: so depraved is Rufa that she steals the offerings of food burnt with the dead to sustain them on their way to the Underworld.

laid...cremator: the undertaker's slave who burnt the corpses i.e. the lowest of the low. His head might be half-shaven to show he was a runaway, adding to Rufa's disgrace. The verb *tundere* literally means 'to beat' or 'to strike' but seems to be a sexual euphemism (Adams, 2002: 148). The verb *pertundere* also appears in the last line of No.25.

29: Insatiable Maecilia: To Cinna

when Pompey was consul: in the year 70 BC.

Cinna: another poet, Catullus' close friend, he also appears in Nos.58 & 88.

he's in again: Pompey's second consulship was 55 BC – the year this poem was composed?

Maecilia: some scholars emend the name to 'Mucilla', a diminutive of Mucia, the name of Pompey's wife and divorced by him in 62 BC, allegedly for adultery with Julius Caesar.

adultery breeds: Maecilia's adulterous band of lovers has grown like seed, a pun in Latin, as in English, on *semen*.

30: Bibulous Postumia: A Drinking Song

fine old Falernian: vintage Falernian was considered one of the best Roman wines, needing ten to twenty years to mature.

Postumia...our tipple-mistress: Roman feasts would always have a 'master of ceremonies' who called toasts and decided on the strength of wine, although given the strictures against women drinking, considered by Pliny the Elder only slightly less sinful than adultery (*Natural History*, 14.89), it is a deliberate shock to find a Roman matron doing the honours. Some have identified Postumia as the wife of Servius Sulpicius Rufus, a friend of Cicero, whose grand-daughter, Sulpicia, was the erotic woman poet (see Balmer, 1996).

diluting waters: wine in classical times was rarely drunk neat.

pure Bacchus...hundred per cent proof: Bacchus, or Dionysus, was god of poetic inspiration as well as of wine.

31: A Wild Woman: an acrostic

acrostic: Goold (2001: 248) points out that the first and last letters of the Latin lines spell out an acrostic, *natu ceu aes:* 'by birth [as hard] as bronze' – a coincidence, perhaps, but still a challenge no translator could pass up.

Scylla: in Latin poetry the sea-monster is usually portrayed as a woman above and barking dogs below.

32: A Cheating (and Pugnacious) Pimp

ten grand: ten thousand *sesterces* is also the price Ameana asks in No.26.

33: Naso's Greatness

split your crack: the Latin verb *scindere* literally means 'to split' but was also slang for anal sex (see Adams, 2002: 150).

34: A Familiar Tale

This fragment might refer to Catullus' male beloved Juventius, which leads us to:

III Loving Juventius (and Hating Furius and Aurelius)

35: Juventius' Kisses

honey eyes...three hundred thousand times...kiss-kiss-kisses: the poem echoes the language and imagery of the Lesbia poems (see Nos.1, 2 & 4).

36: Furious and Aurelius' Disapproval

Aurelius and Furius: the 'close friends' of No.9 return, although here they, rather than Lesbia, are on the receiving end of Catullus' sexually-charged invective.

Bugger off and get stuffed: the same threat Catullus makes to the regulars at the inn in No.6, although here the Latin verb *irrumare* ('to mouth fuck') is joined – in an elegant chiasmus – by *pedicare* ('to bugger').

'million kisses': Catullus' Latin quotes directly from No.1, referring to the counting out of Lesbia's kisses, although as Aurelius and Furius are also seen as rivals for Juventius' favours, it would seem that the implied criticism is of the language of poem No.35 as well.

37: Juventius' Betrayal

rots in rotten borough Pisaurum: on the Adriatic in Umbria, renowned for its unhealthy climate. As for Catullus' rival, the man from Pisaurum, like Coleridge's man from Porlock, is unknown.

peakier than peeling bronze: i.e. from a gilded statue. As Godwin points out, paleness is also seen as a sign of sexual excess (1999: 197).

39: Juventius Adds Insult to Injury

the man who has neither slave nor cash: i.e. Furius, as identified in No.38.

40: Furius' Security

secured...draft: the poem opens and end with two puns; *oppositus*, could mean both 'situated' and 'mortgaged', while *pestilens* or 'plague-ridden', was used of anything unpleasant but particularly of winds, thought to carry plagues.

41: Catullus' Agony

honey-boy: as of Lesbia's sparrow in No.4 (see note on No.35).

on the cross...crucify: as in Nos.21 & 22.

hellebore: a bitter antidote to Juventius' honey-kisses. Godwin notes that the plant was used to treat insanity in the ancient world and so could cure the madness of passion (1999: 211).

42: Hands off Aurelius I

pack your back passage with...mullets...and radish: in antiquity the punishment meted out by husbands to their wives' lovers (Aristophanes, *Clouds*, 1083 & Juvenal 10.314-7).

43: Hands off Aurelius II

cravings: the Latin noun *esuritio* technically refers to starvation, but also means sexual cravings; sexual activity was thought to make its practitioners thin (see Gellius in No.77).

stiff mouth-stuffing...trap stuffed: more *irrumare* (see notes on Nos.6, 36 & 75).

IV Love, Requited

A short section!

44: The Ballad of Septimius and Acme

Acme: a Greek name meaning 'peak' or 'zenith'.

Libya...lion: as in No.31.

sneezed consent: a sneeze was a sign of good omen, although Quinn sees Cupid's response as ironic 'stifling his mirth at the lovers' innocence' (1996: 226).

burning through...my bones: the image of love as a fire in the bones was first used in Sappho 31, a poem Catullus translates in No.5 (see also Balmer, 1992: 38).

Britain, Syria: in 55 BC Caesar invaded Britain, and fellow general Crassus marched on Syria, with rather less success.

V *Good Friends*

45: A Dinner Invitation

salt: a pun on *sal*, both table salt and risqué wit. See note on No.15.

serve our love neat: wine was usually watered with wine (see note on No.30) but, Catullus jokes, in his house love will be undiluted.

scent: the essence of Catullus' beloved, rather than her perfume.

Loves and Cupids: see note on No.4.

sniff it up...become all horn: the Latin *nasus*, or 'nose', could be used as a sexual innuendo; ancient caricatures in graffiti often depicted phallic noses (Adams, 2002: 35).

46: A Welcome Return

Iberia: in No.62, Catullus mentions the fine Spanish linen napkins he has been sent by Veranius and Fabullus.

close those lips with mine: a gentle gibe at Veranius' loquaciousness, perhaps?

47: Flavius' Secret Love

febrile: the Latin *febriculosus* means 'feverish' although perhaps not in the sense of 'hot' but 'feeble' or 'pasty-faced' (Goold, 2001: 39) – this paleness could also indicate her sexual voraciousness (see note on No.43).

tart: the colloquial term *scortum* literally meant a 'skin' or 'hide'.

48: Keeping the Secret: to Cornelius

Cornelius: probably a different Cornelius to Cornelius Nepos in the dedicatory poem.

Horus: the Egyptian sun-god (called by his Greek name Harpocrates in the Latin text) is represented in art as a young boy with a finger pressed to his lips.

49: Caelius (and Quintius) in Love

Caelius: perhaps not the same Caelius to whom Catullus complains of Lesbia's indiscretions in No.20.

Quintius: see note on No.16.

Aufillena: the girl who reneged on a promise in No.27. Her brother Aufillenus appears only here.

keeping it in the family: see Section IX.

in the fire...passion's flames: often seen as a reference to Catullus' traumatic love for Lesbia (although the phrase is echoed by Acme's declaration of love for Septimius in No.44 and also appears in No.52 of Caecilius' poetry-loving girlfriend). However, as Godwin points out (1999: 211), it could also refer to a previous love-affair – possibly one Catullus had had with Caelius, in which case:

in this love plough your own furrow: could be an affectionate dig at Caelius' passive role in his sexual relationship with the poet.

50: Searching for Camerius I

Campus Minimus: unknown but starts a trawl through public places in Rome.

Circus Maximus: where chariots raced, Ben-Hur style.

temple of highest Jove: on the Capitol, rebuilt in 69 BC.

Greatest Pompey's portico: next to the Theatre of Pompey on the Campus Martius, the portico was apparently a good place to pick up girls (Ovid, *The Art of Love*, 1.67). Catullus' deference here to the powerful general C. Pompeius Magnus is almost certainly satirical, ironically placing him just after Jove in ascending order of importance (he is rather more open with his insults in No.91).

Camerius: it has been suggested (Copley, 1952) that the name is a pun on the Greek word *kamarion*, apparently meaning a form of brassière – unlikely, most agree.

51: Searching for Camerius II

Another flying fragment, which may or may not belong with No.50; the tone is certainly very different as Catullus switches from tongue-in-cheek farce to mock heroics, presenting an exhaustive list of strong and swift mythological figures, who nevertheless can't help him overcome his exhaustion from his search for his friend.

52: Caecilius' Epic Love

the love poet: apart from his appearance here and in No.85, Caecilius, possibly an ancestor of Pliny, is unknown.

mistress of Dindymus: Cybele, the *Magna Mater* or 'Great Mother' on whom Caecilius' epic is based. Dindymus is her sacred mountain in Phrygia.

flames have gnawed her to the marrow: the imagery of love as a fire was first found in Sappho (see Nos.3, 44 & 49 and 79), although here it is as much Caecilius' skill as a poet than as a lover that inflames his girl.

as well versed as Sappho: picking up the above imagery – and reminding us of Catullus' own translation of the poem (see No.5).

53: Writing Poems with Licinius Calvus

Licinius: Catullus' great friend, C. Licinius Macer Calvus, was a fellow poet, as well as a renowned orator.

my back pages: the Latin *versiculi*, 'little verses', is a self-deprecating diminutive; the verb *ludere*, 'to play', thought to have been used as a technical term for writing light poetry, also has sexual overtones (Adams, 2002: 162).

swapping rolls: i.e of papyri – but an English innuendo seemed irresistible here.

inflamed: the idea of poetry as sexually arousing also appears in No.52, although here it is the writing as well as the reading of verse which sets the pulse racing.

54: Calvus' Stature

gallery at court: the practice of law was regarded as a spectator sport at Rome.

Calvus talked: Calvus was particularly famous for his prosecution of Caesar's cohort Vatinius in 54 BC (although Cicero's defence actually won the day). Seneca tells the story that during Calvus' speech, Vatinius leapt up and protested 'should I be condemned because he is so eloquent?' (*Declamations*, 7.4.7).

little prick...expound: Calvus might mean 'baldy' but he was also famously short. The Latin *salaputium* is apparently a slang word, although it appears only here and as a proper name on a later inscription, interpreted by Adams as a euphemism for penis (2002: 65).

VI *Bad Poets*
55: Calvus' Prank
Calvus: see Nos.53-54.

hate of Vatinius: the ally of Caesar prosecuted by Calvus in 54 BC (see note on No.54 above).

client: Catullus assumes, probably as a wilful tease, that the collection of *bad* poetry has been sent to Calvus by one of his clients in payment.

Sulla: otherwise unknown, although also the name of the famous Roman general and reforming politician who died in 78 BC.

schoolmaster...setting these texts: the Latin *litterator* means both 'schoolmaster' and 'literary critic'.

Saturnalia: a Roman festival and holiday beginning on 17 December, a day on which jokes were played and gifts were given. By coincidence, this translation was written between 16 and 18 December 2002.

Caesius...Aquinus...Suffenus: a rollcall of supposedly bad poets. Suffenus also appears in No.56.

bad feet limp away: the Latin has the same metrical pun on *pes*, 'a foot'.

56: Suffenus' Delusions: to Varus
Suffenus: see No.55.

Varus: a friend of Catullus, see No.88.

scraps...Royal Leaf: paper was extremely expensive so Catullus and friends such as Varus write their verse on a *palimpsestum* – scrapped and reused papyrus – but the elegant Suffenus uses fine *cartae regiae* or 'royal leaf', probably a technical term for the largest and best-quality paper.

red ribbon...embossed...well-tooled: again, only the best will do for Suffenus; his papyrus rolls are neatly tied, with fine rod-bosses and manuscript covers.

ruled with lead: paper was ruled by lines using a circular piece of lead to keep the writing straight.

pumice finely smoothed: as with Catullus' own book (see note on 'Dedication'), Suffenus uses pumice stone to smooth the ends of his papyrus roll.

baggage that's on our own backs: the Latin refers to one of Aesop's fables in which Zeus gives men two *manticae*, or 'knapsacks', one to be carried on our front, containing the faults of others, one on our backs, containing our own shortcomings, the point being that we are far better at seeing others' faults than our own.

57: Recovering from Reading Sestius' Speech
Sabinum or Tibur: Catullus' country retreat just outside Rome seems to be halfway between the fashionable Tibur (modern Tivoli) and the not so smart Sabinum area. Even in ancient Rome, it seems, a few miles could make all the difference when it came to social pretensions.

Sestius: probably Publius Sestius, a fusty senator, whom even Cicero deemed a bore (*Letters to His Friends*, 7.32.1).

Support-Antius-Now speech: Antius, otherwise unknown, is described here as a *petitor* – a seeker of public office – whose candidature Sestius is supporting.
pestilence-ridden...cold: dull rhetoric was termed *frigidus*, perhaps for its effect on its audience, while in Aristophanes' play *Acharnians*, the poet Theognis freezes over rivers with his bad verse (138-140). Catullus continues this comic tradition, catching cold from Sestius' turgid speech – a joke English idiom can support.

58: One Good Poet to Three Bad

Cinna: the poet friend, to whom No.29 is addressed, now appears in his own poem.
Smyrna: judging by its title, Cinna's poem, which had taken nine years to write, told of the passion of the Cyprian Smyrna (or Myrrha) for her own father, Cinyras, a tale which also appears in Ovid's *Metamorphoses* (10.298-528).
Hortensius: probably Q. Hortensius Hortalus, a florid orator. However, he was known to be sympathetic to Catullus; in No.82, Catullus sends Hortalus a letter accompanying one of his translations of Callimachus, prompting suggestions that the manuscript here might be corrupt. Of Hortensius' great volume of work only one word survives. There is a missing line in Catullus' own poem here.
Volusius' Annals: these terrible documents reappear in No.60.
Cyprus...Po: while Cinna's work will be renowned around the ancient world, Volusius' ramblings won't travel beyond the River Po in northern Italy.
Antimachus: a Greek epic poet, his work became proverbial for wordiness and was reviled as 'fat and inelegant' by Catullus' hero, the Hellenistic poet Callimachus.
short masterpiece...inflated art: a neat summary of the poetic values of Catullus and friends: less is always more.

59: Catullus Bad, Cicero Good

Most eloquent...Cicero: the renowned orator was lavish in his praise of paying clients – as well as of his own talents. Godwin sees the poem as a parody of such 'hyperbolic oratory' (1999: 168).
our best public defender: in 56 BC Cicero had prosecuted Vatinius, although in 54 BC, he successfully defended him against Catullus' friend Calvus (see Nos.54-55). Commentators have seen Catullus' comments as a sly dig at Cicero's ability to change sides.

60: Even Bad Poets Have Their Uses

Volusius' Annals: as mentioned in No.58.
shit-smeared sheets: in No.58 Catullus suggest the poems should be used to wrap fish, here he has an even worse suggestion.
Loves and Cupids: see note on No.4.
iambics: a general term, it would appear, for abusive verse (although this poem is actually written in hendecasyllables), usually written in the metre (see also No.105).
worst of poets: cheekily quoting Catullus' own ironic self-assessment from No.59.
limp-footed Lord / of fire: i.e. the lame god Vulcan, blacksmith of the gods

and cuckolded husband of Venus. The Latin adjective *tardipes* –'slow-footed' – is another metrical pun (see No.55).

O Venus: the poem now becomes a mock-heroic prayer to the goddess of love, invoking many of her shrines, east and west.

61: Battle Lines

hendecasyllables: the eleven-syllable metre (also known as 'Phalaecian') in which the poem is written. The poet assembles feet, lines and verse like military forces; Goold points to the Roman custom for the aggrieved to marshal henchmen to help wreak revenge on their enemies – as Lesbia did when she arranged for the rape of a discarded lover (Goold, 2001: 244, also see Introduction p.17). In No.62, Catullus makes the same threat to the napkin-thief Asinius.

struts like a slut: Cicero said the same of Clodia (*Caelius*, 49).

laughs like she's in some farce: comic actresses were not considered respectable; Cicero was appalled to attend a society dinner-party and find his host's actress mistress sharing the table (*Letters to Friends*, 9.26.2.).

Gallic dog...and my feet: it is surely no coincidence that the Latin noun for dog here – *catulus* – echoes the poet's own name, hence the pun in the English line. Dogs, thought to be sexually shameless, were used as a symbol of insatiable women (see No.31), while Gallic hounds were apparently especially ugly.

VII *The Linen Thieves*

Linen was an expensive commodity in ancient Rome and at dinner parties guests, who ate with their hands, would bring their own napkin to wipe their fingers, while bathers at the Baths would carry their own towels.

62: Asinius' Dinner-party Tricks

Asinius Marrucinus: the Marrucini came from the Adriatic coast.

Pollio: the distinguished historian, C. Asinius Pollio, famed for his account of the Civil Wars of 60-42 BC.

one talent: a handy pun in English, a Greek talent was a very large sum of money (apparently Latin had no such term of its own).

aide-memoire: Catullus uses a Greek word, *mnemosynum* – the only time the word appears in Latin – hence the French expression in its translation.

Fabullus: the dinner-guest from No.45, He later appears with Veranius in Nos.89-90, as they return, empty-handed, from their service in Spain.

Saetaban towels: according to Pliny the Elder, this was the finest linen in Europe (*Natural History*, 19.9); Saetabis is modern Jativa in Tarragon.

63: Thallus Turns More Tricks

Thallus: otherwise unknown – perhaps a pun on *phallus*, picked up by:

bum-boy...soft...bunny's fur: cuniculus or 'rabbit' could also be a pun on a slang word for diarrhoea (see Adams, 2002: 239).

Saetaban towels: see No.62.

Bithynian inlay: presumably brought back by Catullus from his time serving in Bithynia, despite protestations that he came home empty-handed (see Nos.88-89). It isn't clear exactly what this inlay is but the idea of being marked up is picked up in:

shamed...burning, branding whips: Thallus will be flogged as if a slave.

toss this way, that: the Latin puns on the verb *aestuare*, 'to burn', used of pain, as well as of a raging sea; in keeping with the tone of the poem, English can add a touch of sexual innuendo as well.

VIII *Not Such Distinguished Features*

65: Egnatius' Teeth

Egnatius: the dreaded hairy Spaniard of No.6 returns – with his teeth.

supporting the accused: i.e. as a spectator.

Sabine...Tiburtine: see note on No.57.

Umbrian...Etruscan...Lanuvine: Catullus rattles through areas of provincial Italy and their local characteristics.

Transpadane: Catullus' home-town of Verona was in Transpadane Gaul, north of the River Po.

Iberian: on this astonishing national trait see No.6.

66: Arrius' Haitches

Arrius' Haitches: unlike Greek, Latin originally didn't aspirate initial vowels but the habit was becoming fashionable in Catullus' day (*arena*, for example, became *harena*). In the Greek fashion, too, aspirates were also added mid-word so that *pulcer* ('pretty') became *pulcher*, and presumably pronounced with an exaggerated 'h'. Arrius, however, a social climber and Roman Mrs Malaprop, gets it all very wrong. He might possibly be the orator Q. Arrius, known for his ranting style and cited by Cicero as a fine example of a self-made man (*Brutus*, 242).

hadvantages...hartifice: Catullus uses the nonsense words *chommoda* for *commoda* ('advantages') and *hinsidias* for *insidias* ('plots' or 'snares').

Ionian: perhaps a pun on the Greek adjective *chioneous* ('snowy' or 'chilly'), and the Greek dipthong 'ch', playing on a double-meaning of 'rough', as in pronunciation and in seas.

67: The Curse of Rufus' Armpits

Rufus: has been identified with Lesbia/Clodia's lover, Caelius Rufus (perhaps also the Caelius of No.20), he also appears, by inference, in No.68, and as a treacherous friend in No.103.

goat: in classical times, as today, goats were considered randy (see note on No.6).

68: Rufus' Contagion Starts to Spread

goat-pit syndrome: a reference to No.67, but this time the would-be lover isn't the vile-smelling Rufus but a rival.

gout-feet: in No.67 there is no mention of Rufus' gout – perhaps it appears in a lost poem?

stopping play: as Godwin points out, *secare*, the Latin verb here, usually means 'to cut' or 'to wound', but can also mean 'to castrate' (1999: 185).

tainted, infected, by your traces: both the goat-arm and the gout feet are characterised as venereal diseases, transmitted from Rufus to his girl and from her to his unnamed rival.

huge swelling: the Latin puns on *perire* 'to perish (with love)' which was also used of sexual arousal/orgasm (Adams, 2002: 159).

69: Aemilius' Mouth (and Arse)

Aemilius: otherwise unknown.

sesquipedal: the Latin *sesquipedalis* was originally a technical term of measurement for a foot and a half (used by Caesar in *Gallic Wars*, 4.17) but came to stand for any exaggerated size; Horace uses it of long convoluted words (*Art of Poetry*, 97) and Martial of a well-endowed penis (7.14.9). Here, with advanced gum-disease, Aemilius' teeth appear monstrously big.

rotted wheel: the meaning of the Latin noun *ploxenum* (a dialect word from the Po, according to ancient commentators) is obscure; it has been explained as a wagon-box or carriage body whose leather cover is rotting away from the frame, but wagon wheel-spokes seemed more visually apt here.

cunt: the only appearance of female genitalia in Catullus. See Introduction p.21.

donkey-work on treadmill: runaway or disobedient slaves were sent to mills for punishment of turning the pole around the millstone, work usually done by donkeys – here picking up the vivid imagery of the preceding lines.

70: Victius' Tongue

Victius: in the manuscripts, this name also appears as Viccius or Vittius. It has been suggested that he might be the infamous perjurer L. Vettius.

71: Gellius' Lips I

Gellius: sometimes identified as L. Gellius Poplicola, known for his indiscriminate choice of sexual partners (see note on Nos.75-79).

shattered balls: the Latin verb *rumpere* echoes the charge Catullus makes of Lesbia in No.9.

Victor: of Gellius' unfortunate lover nothing else is known.

72: Gellius' Lips II

Another 'floating fragment' thought to belong here; again, as in Nos.3, 5, & 51, there seems to be a sharp change of tone from the low obscenity of No.71 to high moral outrage.

IX   *Incest Isn't Best*

73: Aufillena's Adultery

Aufillena: see Nos.27 & 49.

74: Uncle Gallus' Family Ties

Gallus: otherwise unknown, possibly a misspelling of Gellius (see Nos. 76-79)?

uncles: proverbially stern figures in Rome.

75: Gellius' Uncle (and Aunt)

Gellius: the fellatio-loving anti-hero of No.71 returns with a whole new catalogue of sexual misdemeanours.

uncle: see note on No.74 above.

fuck...mouth: on the Latin verb *irrumare*, see notes on Nos.6 & 36.

76: Gellius' Other Relations

mother, sister itch: L. Gellius Poplicola, with whom Gellius has been tentatively identified, was accused of having an affair with his stepmother.

denying uncle marital rights: see No.75.

far Ocean: in Greek tragedy, the sea often washes away foul crimes (e.g.

Sophocles' *Ajax*, 654-56). Here it is characterised both as a natural object and as its god, Oceanus.

remote wife and daughters: the nymph Tethys and the Oceanids.

opened legs, and swallowed: Gellius' energetic interest in fellatio is known from No.71, although this would be an extremely athletic feat.

77: More of Gellius' Relations

lost weight...emaciated...thin: sexual desire was thought to make one thin (see note on No.43).

78: Gellius' Offspring

Magus begat...Gellius and Mum: according to common belief, the holy men of Persia indulged in incest (Strabo, 17.735).

son's son: the office of Magus was hereditary.

separate grease from grist: i.e. melt the caul away from sacrificial animals' intestines in order to read their entrails for purposes of divination – a solemn task but also a nasty, greasy job, worthy of Gellius' offspring.

79: Catullus' Relations with Gellius

neither mother, sister, to you: another jibe at Gellius' apparent sexual pre-dilections.

the woman whose love gnaws me to the marrow: often seen as a reference to Lesbia. The phrase reoccurs of Acme's love for Septimius in No.44, of Caecilius' girlfriend's arousal by his poetry in No.52 and of an unknown affair in a poem to Caelius (No.49), possibly a reference to Lesbia again or perhaps to a liaison with Caelius himself.

X *In Mourning*

80: To Calvus in Time of Grief

Calvus: on Catullus' great friend, the orator and poet Licinius Calvus, see Nos.53-55.

Quintilia: the later poet Propertius records that Calvus wrote an elegy to his dead wife Quintilia (2.34.89-90), and two surviving fragments of Calvus' poetry are now thought to have come from this work (15 & 16).

81: A Brother's Death

Catullus' unnamed brother, as we learn from No.82, had died on the Hellespont, somewhere near Troy. The poem takes the form of a Greek funerary epigram, although, as Godwin points out, the emphasis is very much on Roman familial traditions and duty (1999: 212).

many the seas, many the lands: it has been suggested that Catullus' visit to his brother's grave took place while the poet was on his way to serve in Bithynia in 57 BC (see Nos.87-89). The journeys of both the poet and previously his brother to the east has also led some to suggest that Catullus' family might have been in business tax-farming in the province (see Goold, 2001: 2).

82: A Letter to Hortalus

Hortalus: probably the orator Q. Hortensius Hortalus, who appears in rather more unflattering light as a long-winded writer in No.58.

Lethe: a river in the Underworld, which washed the cares of the world from the dead.

brother: see No.81.

will I ever: a lost line, with this suggestion supplied by (rare) editorial consensus.

Procne...Itys: Procne's husband Tereus raped her sister Philomela, whose tongue he then cut out to stop her from revealing his crime; when Procne discovered the truth she murdered their son Itys, cooking him and serving him up to his father at a feast. Taking pity on the tragic family, the gods then turned the sisters into birds, a nightingale and a swallow.

translation of Callimachus: the scholarly and often wilfully obscure Alexandrian Greek lyric poet from Cyrene (*c.* 305-240 BC) was a great influence on Catullus. The translation which accompanied the letter is often assumed to be the long mythological poem which follows it in the manuscript (Catullus 66), although the beautiful extended simile following on here could also be a version of a Greek original (see note on No.9).

83: A Reply to Manlius' Request for Love Poems

Manlius: unknown, but writing from Rome, it seems, asking Catullus to send him some new love-poems and to urge the poet to return to the city from a self-imposed exile of grief in Verona.

put on man's toga: at the age of 15 or 16, Roman boys ceremoniously assumed a white toga, signifying their entry into adulthood.

bittersweet goddess: an image from Sappho fragment 130 (see Balmer, 1992: 32).

XI *Home and Away*

84: A Tale of Old Verona

Colonial town: assumed to be Catullus' own home-town of Verona.

second-hand: the Latin *redivivus* was apparently a technical builders' term for recycled planks of wood.

Leaping Leg-Over nights: the Latin refers to the rites of 'Salisubsalus', an obscure term, occurring only here, which has been variously interrupted as a cult title for the god Mars, a reference to some obscure local god, or a 'leaping festival' derived from the verb *salire*, 'to leap' (for whose sexual overtones see note on No.6).

a certain of my townsmen: if Catullus had a particular neighbour in mind, his identity is now obscure – along with many of the nuances of the jokes here.

goat-kid: goats were seen as sexually voracious (see Nos.6 & 67).

Ligurian axe: Liguria, to the west of Verona, was a densely forested area.

no deep stirring in the limbs: see also Nos.36 & 63.

steel horseshoe: Roman horses wore leather slip-on shoes with metal soles that could come off in thick mud – our equivalent would be a horse-shoe imprint.

mule: in No.17, Lesbia's cuckolded husband is described as an ass.

85: A Doorstep Gossip in Verona

This poem is Catullus' version of the Hellenistic epigrams in which inanimate objects speak; doors also played an important role in Greek and Latin love-poetry and drama, preventing star-crossed lovers from meeting, for example. The gossipy slaves of ancient comedy also provide a model for the door's character.

Balbus: unknown.

pegged-out: the Latin *porrectus* or 'stretched-out' was used colloquially of the dead.

Caecilius: probably Catullus' epic-writing friend from No.52.

Brixia...Cycnus...Mella: Brixia, modern Brescia, appears to have been the bride's home-town, sited beneath Cycnus hill and its look-out tower on the Mella river. Goold suggests these grandiose geographical details might be typical of Veronese scorn at a rival town's pretensions (2001: 256).

Cornelius...Postumus affair: neither are known. The name Postumus, here used adjectivally with *amore* ('love-affair'), could well be a pun.

one more name: again, the 'tall man's' identity isn't known, although it has been suggested that it might be Caecilius, whom Catullus is again teasing for his colourful love-life.

sued...case of the missing pregnancy: i.e. a paternity suit bought by the wife against this unnamed lover, dropped when no pregnancy materialised.

86: Catullus' Yacht

The Latin *phaselus*, a craft used by rich Romans for pleasure cruising, was named after the Greek for 'bean-pod' due to its shape. A later Latin parody of this poem, about a mule-driver called Sabinus, still survives.

you see there: Catullus could be showing guests the actual ship or a model, a votive offering on an altar (Goold, 2001: 237).

Adriatic...islands Cycladic...Rhodes...Propontis...Pontus: the poem travels backwards through the journey from the yacht's origins in the forests of Bithynia to Catullus' villa at Sirmio on Lake Garda in north Italy.

Amastris, Cytorus: towns on the Black Sea, a wooded area, known for their forestry.

palms: a play on oar-palms and of the hand, personifying the yacht, as throughout.

sailors' guardians: the constellation of Gemini helped sailors navigate. During excavations at Sirmione on Lake Garda (see No.87) – a site still known locally as 'the grotto of Catullus' – a head of one of the Gemini was discovered.

87: Home, At Last, From Bithynia

Sirmio: the peninsula of Sirmione on Lake Garda where Catullus seems to have had a family villa.

back from the plains of Thynia / and Bithynians: in 57 BC. Catullus had had a wretched time serving in Bithynia, a Roman province of Asia Minor, under the governor C. Memmius (for more on which see Nos.88-89). Catullus throws in some mock-learned geographical forms here, including the almost obsolete *Thyniam* for the province and playing with the Latin prefix *bi-*.

Gardian lake: in the Latin Catullus calls the lake *Lydiae* or 'Lydian', usually explained as a reference to local Etruscans, believed to have originated in the east, although the text has been disputed. Godwin sees the joke as the waters being as much home from a long journey as Catullus (1999: 148), but English offered an irresistible pun here.

wave...roar...feel it in your waters: Catullus plays on the traditional literary image of rippling water being like laughter.

88: Never As Much As We Might Say...

Varus: also appears as the addressee of No.56; he has been identified with both Alfenus Varus, a leading politician (in which case he could also be the Alfenus of No.101) and Quintilius Varus, a literary critic mourned by Horace in *Odes* 1.24.

Bithynia: see note on No.87. The action of the poem takes place after Catullus' return from the province.

get palms oiled: the Latin expression *caput unctius referre* or 'bring back an oiled head' meant having something to celebrate, or colloquially 'get richer', and apparently referred to the habit of oiling heads on holiday celebrations (Godwin, 1999: 126). Cicero used the same phrase of Verres, the corrupt governor of Sicily (*Against Verres*, 2.2.54).

mouth-fucker praetor: C. Memmius, governor of Bithynia in 57 BC, was known for his fairness towards his colonial population, stopping the corruption and self-advancement that usually characterised Roman provincial service. His benevolence towards provincials, however, was apparently seen as gross misconduct towards his staff; judging by Catullus' indignation here, profiting from provincial service seems to have been regarded as a right rather than a shady perk. Once again he uses the term *irrumator* (see also Nos.6, 36, 43 & 72); the opposite and inverse insult to our 'cock-sucker'.

litter-bearers: Bithynia was actually known for its wooden litters, made, like Catullus' yacht in No.86, from its famous high-quality timber.

Serapis: i.e. the temple of the Egyptian healing deity.

Cinna, that is Caius: possibly the poet of No.58, who, it has been suggested, might have accompanied Catullus to Bithynia. In his embarrassment, Catullus stutters out his friend's name backwards.

89: ...Or We Might Hope

Piso: presumably L. Calpurnius Piso, father-in-law of Julius Caesar and governor of Macedonia in 57-55 BC, although in No.62, Fabullus and Veranius are together in Spain and in No.46, Catullus welcomes Veranius back from Spain. Presumably they went abroad on colonial service more than once, like many noble young men climbing up the Roman political rungs or so-called *cursus honorum*.

travelling light, backs unpacked: Catullus puns on the meaning of *cohors*, imagining his friends not just as Piso's staff but his troop of soldiers; the Latin *sarcinulae* were the half-emptied knapsacks carried by light infantry on the march.

glass-rim scum: Catullus uses the word *vappa*, meaning 'flat wine', which according to Merrill was a colloquialism for 'good for nothing'.

Memmius: C. Memmius, governor of Bithynia in 57 BC, under whom Catullus served as a member of his cohorts. For Catullus' grudge against his boss see note on No.88.

fucked me up: irrumare again (see No.88).

no less renowned a prick: i.e. Piso. *Verpa* was an extremely vulgar term, found more in graffiti than in literature (Adams, 2002: 13).

has stuffed you both: not the obscene *irrumare* for once but the rather more restrained *fartus* or 'stuffed'. Adams has discovered that, as in English idiom, the verb was used in a sexual context, usually of oral sex (2002: 139).

Forge favourable friendships: the Latin seems to be a tag quoted, perhaps, by fathers to sons. Catullus' rejection of the advice here isn't just a comic fit of pique; his poetry contains few references to the public political life wealthy young Romans would engage in as a matter of course. See Introduction p.14.

founding fathers: Romulus and Remus, the brothers who, in Latin legend, founded Rome.

90: The Grass Is Always Greener

Porcius...Socration: possibly C. Porcius Cato, tribune in 56 BC, and the philosopher Philodemus, whose nickname was 'little Socrates' after the Athenian philosopher. The names are apt, as Godwin comments (1999: 166), bringing to mind images of avariciousness and feasting.

theft-hand: in Latin *sinistrae* or 'left-hand' – the hand thought to be used for wrong-doing.

prick Piso: see on No.89.

plague and privation: see note on Aurelius in No.43 and on Gellius in No.77.

Veranius and Fabullus: see No.89 above.

91: To Pompey and Julius Caesar: In Protest at Mamurra's Greed

Pompey...Julius Caesar: the two greatest generals – and most powerful men – of their day. The two later fought a civil war, which Caesar won.

Mamurra: a wealthy protégée of Caesar and Pompey, who, as we learn here, had served under Pompey in the eastern campaigns against Mithridates of 66-63 BC, and apparently gained his riches in Caesar's subsequent campaigns in Spain, Gaul and Britain.

spoils of remote Britannia: in 55 BC, after a string of successful campaigns in Spain and Gaul, Caesar had invaded Britain – an invasion also referred to by Catullus in No.9.

bum-boy: the Greek word *cinaedus* was used of a passive partner in anal sex (see Nos.36, 63 & 95); for Caesar's infamous bisexuality see note on No.97.

remote, far-western island: Britain is also described as *ultima* in No.9.

fucked-out prick: in subsequent poems, *mentula*, or 'prick', becomes Catullus' nickname for Mamurra (Nos.92-94).

reached his peak: the Latin verb *expatrare* literally means 'to plough up' but was also used idiomatically of orgasm (Adams, 2002: 142-43).

Pontus' booty: i.e. in the Mithridatic campaigns with Pompey.

father and son-in-law: Pompey had married Caesar's daughter Julia in 59 BC.

92: Mamurra the Prick

Prick: apparently Mamurra, referred to as a *mentula* in No.91.

expenses exceed yield: on Mamurra's legendary profligacy see note on Nos.91 & 93.

let him be rich: a typical Catullan paradox; the more Mamurra gains the more he'll have to lose.

93: More Prick

Hyperborea: the legendary kingdom beyond the north wind, with a nice echo of 'hyperbole' here too.

biggest man...biggest prick: a similar joke is used of Naso in No.33.

94: Yet More Prick

Prick: Mamurra now has literary aspirations.

mount Olympus: Olympus was the mountain home of the Greek gods and Pipla, a spring on its slopes, was sacred to the Muses. The Latin verb *scandere*, 'to climb', was used of mounting animals suggesting the pun in English (Adams, 2002: 205).

boil a pot...: in Latin the obscure proverb 'the pot picks its own vegetables' seems to mean that a man will seek what a man needs, i.e. do whatever comes naturally. Adams wonders whether the reference to 'pot' and 'vegetables' also has an obscene *double entendre* (2002: 29).

95: Caesar and Mamurra

bum-boys: as in No.91, Catullus again uses the term *cinaedus*, a passive partner in anal sex (see also Nos.36 & 63 and note on No.91).

catamite: the Latin term *pathicus*, apparently referred specifically to the passive partner in an act of *irrumatio* or 'mouth-fucking' (Quinn, 1996: 144). *Cinaedus* and *pathicus* are also used of Aurelius and Furius in No.36.

Formiae: see Nos.13 &26.

96: Shunning Caesar

what sort of man: in Latin the colloquial 'whether the man is black or white' means 'I don't need to know anything about you'.

97: Annoying Caesar

Catullus produces a list of annoying men to prove that there are far worse sources of irritation for Caesar than the poet's own scurrilous verses.

Otho...knob-head: Otho is unknown; Latin *caput*, 'head', could be applied to a penis (Adams, 2002: 72).

Hirrus: perhaps C. Lucilius Hirrus, a cousin of Pompey.

Libo: possibly L. Scribonius Libo. The other names are obscure.

angered again: Suetonius tells the story that Catullus later apologised for his attacks and was immediately invited to dine with Caesar (*Julius Caesar*, 73). Lampooning Caesar, though, seems to have been a popular pastime among Catullus' set; Suetonius (*op. cit.* 49) quotes a snatch of a poem about Caesar's (homosexual) sex life by Catullus' friend Calvus.

peerless legate: Catullus uses the same phrase (*unice imperator*) of Caesar in No.91.

98: Catullus in Despair

curule's chair: used by those of high office such as praetors and consuls. Nonius isn't known.

Vatinius: Calvus' great enemy (see No.54), was apparently bought a praetorship by Caesar and Pompey in 55 BC, in return for his support, and, as he liked to boast, promised a consulship (Cicero, *Against Vatinius*, 11) – it did not materialise until 47 BC, and then he held office only for a month.

XIII *The Wages of Sin: Betrayals and Recriminations*

99: Love's Punishment: A Joke for Cato

Cato: has been identified as either Catullus' fellow neoteric poet Valerius Cato or perhaps Cato Uticensis, the old-fashioned moralist. If the latter, the poem is a joke at its addressee's expense.

beating his rod: the Latin verb *trusare*, 'to push' could, it seems, refer euphemistically to either intercourse or masturbation – most commentators agree that the latter seems more likely here.

100: Cominius the Informer Gets His Just Desserts

Cominius: otherwise unknown.

101: Alfenus' Betrayal

Written in Greater Asclepiadean metre, an ancient Greek metre consisting of 16 syllable lines based around three choriambs, usually with a break between each one – used by Catullus only here.

Alfenus: possibly Alfenus Varus, a leading politician, and in which case the Varus whose girlfriend catches Catullus out in No.88. The cause of Catullus' grievance here is vague and unknown.

103: Rufus' Poison

Rufus: see Nos.67 & 68.

104: Cornificius' Defection

Cornificius: possibly Quintus Cornificius, a poet and orator, friend of Cicero and supporter of Caesar. The cause of Catullus' dejection here is not clear, although sometimes attributed to his love for Lesbia.

Hercules...laborious: a joking reference to Hercules' famous 12 Labours.

Simonides' dirges: the Greek lyric poet was apparently renowned for the sadness of his poems, so much so that his name might have become synonymous with (perhaps excessively) sorrowful verse.

105: Ravidus' Insanity

Ravidus: otherwise unknown.

iambics: in Catullus, the metre of ridicule and lampoon (see also No.60).

without all due form: unlike Catullus' own mock-formal invocations in No.60.

Endpiece

versions of Callimachus: Catullus also refers to translating Callimachus in No. 82.

Gellius: the depraved and incestuous lover of Nos.71-72, 75-78.

revenge – in verse: again Catullus shows his literary confidence; Godwin points out that the poem – the last in the Catullus manuscript – ends *in mediis rebus*, drawing the reader in and so 'invites us to go back to the beginning and start all over again' (1999: 223). Good idea.

CAST OF CHARACTERS

Acme: lover of Septimius in No.44.

Aemilius: in No.69 gap-toothed and gum-diseased, but still a successful lover – if of rather undiscerning women.

Alfenus: a disloyal friend to Catullus in No.101, possibly the same man as **Varus**.

Ameana: a big-nosed prostitute who overcharges Catullus for her services while dallying with the hated **Mamurra** in Nos.13 & 26.

Antimachus: a Greek epic poet (*c.* 440 BC), reviled for his over-inflated art in No.58.

Antius: a candidate for public office, supported by **Sestius'** bad speech in No.57.

Aquinus: a bad poet, whose work is sent by Catullus to Calvus in No.55, in retaliation for his friend's Saturnalia prank. He might be the writer mentioned by Cicero in *Tusculan Disputations* 5.63.

Arrius: in No.66, a hopeless social climber with an irritating habit of aspirating words, possibly the long-winded orator and self-made man, Q. Arrius.

Asinius Marrucinus: a linen-thief berated by Catullus in No.62, and brother of the renowned historian **Pollio**.

Aufillena: sister of **Aufillenus**. In No.27, a girl who reneges on her promise to sleep with Catullus; in No.49, she is wooed by **Quintius**, although in No.73, she is married but committing adultery with her own uncle.

Aufillenus: a young gentleman of Verona, wooed by **Caelius** in No.49.

Aurelius: in Nos.42 & 43, a rival for Catullus' beloved Juventius, although more usually found in the company of his cohort, **Furius**; in No.36 the pair are attacked in return for their criticisms of Catullus' poetry and in No.9, they're asked to take a message to the unfaithful Lesbia.

Balbus: an old man, previous owner of the door (and house) in No.85.

Caecilius: a love poet from Como who, in No.52, is inflaming the passions of his girlfriend with his work-in-progress, *Magna Mater*. He is also the owner of the house door in No.85.

Caelius Rufus: an orator and ambitious politician, allied with Julius Caesar, who had an affair with Clodia Metelli ('Lesbia?') after her husband's death in 59 BC. When he ended the affair, she had him arraigned on a charge of poison in 56 BC. Caelius was successfully defended by Cicero in one of the orator's most famous speeches. He may be the **Caelius** referred to in No.20, a poem about Lesbia's infidelities, and even the hairy-armpited **Rufus** of Nos.67 & 68, but not:

Caelius: the suitor of Aufillenus in No.49, a native of Verona.

Caesar, Julius (100-44 BC): the famous general and politician, who invaded Britain in 55 BC (see No.9). Although a family friend and a regular guest at Verona, for the most part he is lampooned in scurrilous terms in Catullus' poetry (see Nos.91, 95-97).

Caesius: a bad poet, whose work Catullus collects for Calvus in No.55.

Calvus: C. Licinius Macer Calvus, was Catullus' closest friend, and a fellow poet as well as a distinguished orator (see No.54). In No.53, Catullus and Calvus (meaning 'Baldy') compose erotic verse together, and in No.55, Calvus sends Catullus the worst poetry he can find as a Saturnalia prank. In No.80, Catullus comforts his friend after the death of Quintilia, his young wife or mistress.

Camerius: a friend for whom Catullus searches high and low in No.50 and whose name may or may not be a pun on *kamarion*, a Greek word for a brassière.

Cato: urged by Catullus in No.99 to laugh at one of the poet's recent sexual adventures, identified either as the poet and orator Valerius Cato or Cato Uticensis, an old-fashioned moralist.

Cicero (106-43 BC): the famous orator and writer, who successfully defended **Caelius Rufus** against Clodia's charges in 56 BC. He also coined the expressions *neoteroi* and *novi poetae* for Catullus and his circle of young poets. In No.59, Catullus ironically praises Cicero's skill as an orator.

Cinna: a poet and close friend of Catullus, praised in No.58 for his poem *Smyrna*. No.29, on **Maecilia**'s adultery, is addressed to him, and in No.88, he appears as the true owner of the litter-bearers Catullus has tried to pass off as his own. He might well be the unfortunate C. Helvius Cinna, the poet and tribune torn to pieces after **Caesar**'s murder in 44 BC by an angry mob, who mistook him for the conspirator L. Cornelius Cinna.

Clodia Metelli: sister of **P. Clodius Pulcher**, wife of Metellus Celer and lover of **Caelius Rufus**, she has been identified as the model for Catullus' mistress Lesbia, although this identification is greatly disputed.

Publius Clodius Pulcher: populist political activist, brother of **Clodia**.

Cominius: in No.100, a dirty old man and informer, whom Catullus urges to be repaid with rough justice.

Cornelius: in No.48 a friend urged by Catullus to trust the poet with a secret. The name also occurs in No.85, as an unfaithful wife's lover.

Cornificius: a friend chided by Catullus for his lack of sympathy in No.104. He has been identified with Quintus Cornificius, a poet, orator and general, friend of **Cicero**, and supporter of **Julius Caesar**.

Cornelius Nepos (*c.* 99-*c.* 24 BC): historian, biographer and poet. An elder contemporary of Catullus and, according to **Cicero**, a keen admirer of the younger poet. Catullus' collection is dedicated to Nepos, leading some to believe that he may have collected and edited Catullus' poems after the poet's death. He is not thought to be the same **Cornelius** of Nos.48 & 85.

Egnatius: a hairy, bearded Spaniard with a brilliant smile, achieved, so Catullus claims in Nos.6 & 65, by washing his teeth with his own urine.

Fabullus: friend of Catullus, invited to dine with the poet in No.45. He serves with **Veranius** in Spain from where they send Catullus some fine linen napkins (No.62). The two also serve under **Piso** in Macedonia, with less rewarding gain (Nos.89-90).

Flavius: Catullus' friend with a secret lover – and an exhausting love-life – in No. 47.

Furius: satirised in Nos.38 & 40 for his spendthrift ways and subsequent poverty, he also appears in Nos.9 & 36 with his 'close friend' **Aurelius**. He has been identified with the poet Furius Bibaculus.

Gallus: in No.74, he arranges the incestuous affair of his nephew and sister-in-law.

Gellius: in Nos.75-78, an incestuous lover of aunts, sister and mother, while in No.71, he exhausts **Victor** with his insatiable appetite for fellatio. In No.79, Catullus berates Gellius for his disloyalty as a friend and his collection ends with an account of the poet's rebuffed attempts at reconciliation. He has been identified as L.Gellius Poplicola, known for his indiscriminate choice of sexual partners and accused before the senate of having an affair with his stepmother.

Hirrus: a country bumpkin in No.97, perhaps C. Lucilius Hirrus, a cousin of Pompey.

Hortalus: see **Hortensius** below.

Hortensius: in No.58, a wordy writer, churning out works, identified with the florid orator, Q. Hortensius Hortalus. In No.82, though, Catullus sends Hortalus a friendly letter accompanying one of his translations of Callimachus.

Ipsitilla: a call-girl with whom Catullus wishes to spend the afternoon in No.25.

Juventius: Catullus' male beloved in Nos.35, 37, 39 & 41, and pursued by **Aurelius** in Nos.42-43. According to Cicero, the Iuventii were a distinguished Roman family.

'Lesbia': the name given to Catullus' lover in several poems. She has often been identified with **Clodia Metelli**.

Lesbius: brother of Lesbia in No.14, where he is called 'Pulcher' leading commentators to identify him with **Publius Clodius Pulcher**.

Libo: in No.97, memorable for his annoying flatulence, possibly L. Scribonius Libo.

Licinius: see **Calvus**.

Maecilia: the adulteress whose lovers grow a hundredfold in No.29, identified by some as Pompey's wife Mucia, whom he divorced in 62 BC.

Mamurra ('the Prick'): a wealthy protégée of **Caesar**, who gained his riches, as Catullus complains in No.91, during Caesar's campaigns in Spain, Gaul and Britain. According to Nos.92-93, he also squandered his wealth as quickly as he acquired it. Nicknamed *Mentula*, 'the Prick', by Catullus, he appears as **Ameana**'s lover in Nos.13 & 26.

Manlius: an otherwise unknown friend of Catullus, who in No.83 has apparently urged the poet to send him some love poetry.

Menenius: cuckolded husband of **Rufa** in No.28.

Memmius: C. Memmius, governor of Bithynia in 57 BC, on whose staff Catullus served. He was known for his fairness towards his colonial population, stopping corruption among his staff, much to the poet's annoyance, as voiced in Nos.88-89.

Naso: a promiscuous rent-boy in No.33.

Nonius: a wart-ridden, ambitious politician reviled by a despairing Catullus in No.98.

Otho: in No.97, owner of a small 'knob-head', otherwise unknown but apparently an associate of **Julius Caesar**.

Piso, L. Calpurnius: governor of Macedonia in 57-55 BC, under whom **Veranius** and **Fabullus** serve in Nos.89-90.

Pollio: the distinguished historian C..Asinius Pollio (76 BC – AD 4), praised in No.62, in contrast with his disreputable brother, **Asinius**, the dinner-party linen-thief.

Pompey (106-48 BC): the great Roman general was at first allied with **Julius Caesar**, marrying his daughter Julia in 59 BC, although they later fought a civil war for control of Rome – which Pompey lost. In No.91, Catullus castigates him, with Caesar, for their support of the grasping **Mamurra** and in No.50 satirises his sense of self-grandeur in a passing allusion.

Porcius: a greedy hanger-on of the provincial governor **Piso** in No.90. He has been tentatively identified with C. Porcius Cato, a tribune in 56 BC.

Postumia: mistress of ceremonies in the drinking fest of No.30. She has been identified by some as the wife of Servius Sulpicius Rufus, a friend of **Cicero**, whose grand-daughter, Sulpicia, was one of the few known Roman women poets.

Postumus: an adulterous lover of a young wife of Verona in No.85.

Quintia: appears as a rival beauty to **Lesbia** in No.15, possibly sister of **Quintius.**

Quintilia: the dead wife or mistress of **Calvus** in No.80.

Quintius: a young gentleman of Verona, who appears as a rival to Catullus in No.16 and as a suitor for **Aufillena** in No.49.

Ravidus: in No.105, a disloyal friend, so desperate for fame at any cost that he angers Catullus just to appear in the poet's verses.

Rufa: a Roman matron with a taste for sordid sexual encounters; in No.28, she is married to **Menenius** but performs fellatio on **Rufulus** and sleeps with an undertaker's slave. Perhaps the sister of

Rufus: in Nos.67-68, a would-be seducer whose hairy armpits repel women, and in No.103 a false friend who betrays Catullus' trust. He has been tentatively identified with **Caelius Rufus**.

Rufulus: enjoys **Rufa**'s favours in No.28.

Septimius: besotted lover of **Acme** in No.44.

Sestius: the author of a bad speech in support of **Antius** which gives Catullus a cold in No.57, he might be Publius Sestius, a senator so dull even **Cicero** deemed him a bore.

Silo: a pugnacious pimp in No.32.

Socration: with **Porcius**, a hanger-on of the provincial governor **Piso** in

No.90. He has been tentatively identified with the poet and philosopher Philodemus whose nickname was 'Little Socrates'.

Suffenus: an elegant man-about-town who loves to write poetry, even if, as Catullus claims in No.56, it reads like the work of a 'goat-milker'. He also appears in the roll-call of bad poets Catullus sends **Calvus** in No.55.

Sufficius: in No.97, very elderly, otherwise unknown.

Sulla: a schoolmaster client of **Calvus** in No.55.

Thallus: the towel-thief of No.63.

Varus: the proud owner of a new girlfriend in No.88, he also appears as the addressee of No.56, on **Suffenus'** so-called poetry. He may be Alfenus Varus, a leading politician, and in which case he may also be the **Alfenus** of No.101, or Quintilius Varus, a literary critic mentioned by Horace.

Vatinius: prosecuted by **Calvus** in No.54, although successfully defended by **Cicero**. In No.98, Catullus despairs of a world in which such politicians prosper.

Veranius: a friend of Catullus, in No.46, welcomed back from Spain; and in No.62, with Fabullus, he sends Catullus fine Spanish linen napkins. With **Fabullus**, too, he also serves under **Piso** in Macedonia, with less rewarding gain (Nos.89-90).

Vibennius: a bath-house thief in No.64, father of a rent-boy.

Victius: in No.70, the owner of a foul, wagging tongue.

Victor: in No.71, is exhausted by **Gellius'** insatiable attentions.

Volusius: a terrible, though prolific poet; in No.58, Catullus recommends using his books for fish-wrapping and in No.60 likens them to used toilet paper.

GLOSSARY

Adonis: youthful lover of Venus.

Adriatic: sea between Italy and former Yugoslavia.

Amastris: sea-port in Bithynia, on the Black Sea.

Amathus: shrine to Venus on Cyprus.

Ancon: cult centre of Venus in Picenum, Italy.

Bacchus: god of wine and poetic inspiration.

Battus: legendary founder of Cyrene.

Bithynia: Roman province in Asia Minor.

Brixia: northern Italian city on the banks of river Mella, modern Brescia.

Castor and Pollux: the Gemini or Twins.

Cisalpine Gaul: area of northern Italy, Catullus' family home.

Cnidus: city in Caria with many temples to Venus.

Croesus: 6th century BC king of Lydia with legendary wealth.

Cupid: diminutive, arrow-bearing love-god.

Cybele: eastern fertility goddess.

Cycladic islands: large island group to the east of Greece.

Cycnus: hill in Brixia.

Cyrene: city in Libya.

Cytorus: town on the Black Sea, famous for its box-wood.

Dindymus: mountain in Phrygia, sacred to Cybele.

Dyrrachium: port on the Adriatic, in what is now modern Albania.

Etruria: Italian region of N.W. Italy.

Firmum: Italian town on the Adriatic coast in Picenum, now Fermo.

Formiae: town in Campania, south of Rome.

Gaul: Roman province, roughly equivalent to modern France.

Golgi: cult centre of Venus/Aphrodite on Cyprus.

Hellespont: the strait of Dardanelles, at the mouth of the Black Sea.

Hercules: or Heracles, legendary hero, performer of 12 Labours.

Horus (or Harpocrates): Egyptian son-god represented as a young boy with finger on his lips.

Hyperborea: legendary land beyond the sun in the far north.

Iberia: ancient name for Spain.

Idalium: town in Cyprus, with a temple to Venus.

Ionian: sea between Italy and Greece.

Jove: see Jupiter.

Jupiter: king of the Roman pantheon of gods, identified with the Greek god Zeus and the Egyptian deity Ammon.

Itys: murdered by his mother Procne and served up at a feast to his father Tereus, after Tereus had raped his aunt Philomela.

Ladas: Spartan athlete who died after winning a race at Olympia.

Lanuvium: Italian town south of Rome.

Larium: Latin name for Lake Como in northern Italy.

Lethe: river in the Underworld.

Liguria: forested Italian region, north of Rome and west of Verona.

Lydia: territory in Asia Minor, renowned for its wealth.

Mella: river in Brixia.

Midas: legendary king who asked the gods for a golden touch; destroyed by his greed when all he touched, family, clothes, even food, turned to gold.

Muses: nine goddesses of literary and artistic inspiration.

Nemesis: goddess of revenge and reciprocal fair-dealing.

Neptune: Roman sea god.

Novus Comus (or Novum Comum): town on Lake Como.

Olympus: mountain in northern Greece, home of the Greek gods.

Orcus: a name for Pluto, the ruler of the Underworld, transferable to the Underworld itself.

Parthians: eastern tribe who bordered the Roman Empire in Asia Minor, famed for their cavalry archers and backward shots.

Pegasus: mythological winged horse, ridden by the hero Bellerophon.

Perseus: mythological wing-sandaled hero, slayer of Medusa the Gorgon.

Pisaurum: town on the Adriatic, known for its unhealthy climate.

Po: northern Italian river.

Pontus: Black Sea.

Procne: wife of Tereus, who killed their son Itys when she leaned Tereus had raped her sister Philomela. She was later turned into a nightingale.

Propontis: sea of Marmora, between the Hellespont and the Black Sea.

Rhesus: mythological King of Thrace who owned a pair of swift white horses.

Rhodes: island in the eastern Mediterranean.

Romulus and Remus: legendary twins, founders of Rome.

Sabinum: not-so-smart area outside Rome.

Sagae: tribe who lived in the area of modern Tashkent, northern Iran.

Saetabis: Spanish city, modern Jativa in Tarragon, famed for its fine linen.

Saturnalia: Roman festival of jokes, held in late December.

Scylla: sea-monster, half-woman, half-dog.

Serapis: Egyptian healing deity, popular with the lower classes in Rome.

Sirmio: modern Sirmione, a promontory on Lake Garda, where Catullus had a country retreat.

Smyrna (or Myrrha): mythological Cyprian princess who conceived a passion for her own father Cinyras.

Talos: bronze giant who in Greek mythology guarded Crete.

Thynia: see Bithynia.

Tibur: smart area outside Rome, modern Tivoli.

Transpadane: area of Cisalpine Gaul, north of the river Po, in which Catullus' home-town of Verona was sited.

Umbria: region of North East Italy.

Urcanes: tribe from Hyrcania, on the southern shore of the Caspian sea.
Urium: cult-centre of Venus in Apulia, Italy.
Venus: goddess of love, Roman version of Greek Aphrodite.
Verona: northern Italian city, Catullus' home town.
Vulcan: lame blacksmith of the gods, cuckolded husband of Venus.

ANCIENT WRITERS & SOURCES

Aesop: Greek fable-writer, *fl.* 600 BC.
Anacreon: Greek lyric poet, *c.* 570-485 BC.
Apuleius: Roman novelist, born *c.* AD 123.
Archilochus: Greek lyric poet, *fl. c.* 675 BC.
Aristophanes: Athenian comic playwright, *c.* 450-385 BC.
Callimachus: Alexandrian Greek lyric poet from Cyrene, *c.* 305-240 BC.
Diodorus: Graeco-Roman historian, *c.* 60-30 BC.
Herodotus: Greek historian, *c.* 450 BC.
Hipponax: Greek lyric poet, *fl. c.* 540-37 BC.
Horace: Roman poet, 65-08 BC.
Isidore: Bishop of Seville, AD 602-36.
Jerome: Christian theologian, historian and translator, *c.* AD 348-420.
Juvenal:. Roman satirical poet, *fl.* AD 100-18.
Martial: Roman poet, *c.* AD 40-104.
Ovid: Roman poet, 43 BC–AD 17.
Pliny (the elder): Roman writer and natural historian (AD 24-79).
Pliny (the younger): Roman writer, AD 61-*c.* 112.
Propertius: Roman poet, *fl. c.* 25 BC.
Sappho: Greek lyric poet of Lesbos, *fl. c.* 600 BC.
Seneca the Elder: Roman rhetorician and historian, *b.* 55 BC.
Simonides: dirge-like Greek lyric poet, 556-467 BC.
Strabo: Greek geographer, *c.* 63 BC-AD 21.
Suetonius: Roman historian and imperial biographer, *b. c.* AD 69.
Sulpicia: Roman woman elegiac poet, *fl. c.* 1 AD.

KEY TO THE POEMS: I

Poem number	M/S Text number	Poem number	M/S Text number	Poem number	M/S Text number
Frontispiece	14b	35	48	71	80
Dedication	1	36	16	72	78b
1	5	37	81	73	111
2	7	38	23	74	78
3	2	39	24	75	74
4	3	40	26	76	88
5	51	41	99	77	89
6	37	42	15	78	90
7	8	43	21	79	91
8	72	44	45	80	96
9	11	45	13	81	101
10	75	46	9	82	65
11	70	47	6	83	68a
12	87	48	102	84	17
13	43	49	100	85	67
14	79	50	55	86	4
15	86	51	58b	87	31
16	82	52	35	88	10
17	83	53	50	89	28
18	92	54	53	90	47
19	104	55	14	91	29
20	58	56	22	92	114
21	85	57	44	93	115
22	76	58	95	94	105 & 94
23	107	59	49	95	57
24	109	60	36	96	93
25	32	61	42	97	54
26	41	62	12	98	52
27	110	63	25	99	56
28	59	64	33	100	108
29	113	65	39	101	30
30	27	66	84	102	73
31	60	67	69	103	77
32	103	68	71	104	38
33	112	69	97	105	40
34	106	70	98	*Endpiece*	116

KEY TO THE POEMS: II

M/S Text number	Poem number	M/S Text number	Poem number	M/S Text number	Poem number
1	*Dedication*	41	26	82	16
2	3	42	61	83	17
3	4	43	13	84	66
4	86	44	57	85	21
5	1	45	44	86	15
6	47	47	90	87	12
7	2	48	35	88	76
8	7	49	59	89	77
9	46	50	53	90	78
10	88	51	5	91	79
11	9	52	98	92	18
12	62	53	54	93	96
13	45	54	97	94	94
14	55	55	50	95	58
14b	*Frontispiece*	56	99	96	80
15	42	57	95	97	69
16	36	58	20	98	70
17	84	58b	51	99	41
21	43	59	28	100	49
22	56	60	31	101	81
23	38	65	82	102	48
24	39	67	85	103	32
25	63	68a	83	104	19
26	40	69	67	105	94
27	30	70	11	106	34
28	89	71	68	107	23
29	91	72	8	108	100
30	101	73	102	109	24
31	87	74	75	110	27
32	25	75	10	111	73
33	64	76	22	112	33
35	52	77	103	113	29
36	60	78	74	114	92
37	6	78b	72	115	93
38	104	79	14	116	*Endpiece*
39	65	80	71		
40	105	81	37		

SELECTED BIBLIOGRAPHY

J.N. Adams: *The Latin Sexual Vocabulary* (London: Duckworth, 2002).

Josephine Balmer: *Sappho: Poems and Fragments* (Newcastle upon Tyne: Bloodaxe Books, 1992).

————: *Classical Women Poets* (Newcastle upon Tyne: Bloodaxe Books, 1996).

Eva Cantarella: *Bisexuality in the Ancient World*, trs Cormac Ó Cuilleanáin (New Haven & London, Yale Nota Bene, 2002).

F.O. Copley: 'Catullus 55, 9-14', *American Journal of Philology*, 73 (1952), 295-97.

W. Fitzgerald: *Catullan Provocations: Lyric Poetry and the Drama of Position* (Berkeley: University of California Press, 2000).

C.J. Fordyce (ed.): *Catullus* (Oxford: Oxford University Press, 1961).

Julia Haig Gaisser (ed.): *Catullus in English* (London: Penguin, 2001).

Daniel H. Garrison (ed.): *The Student's Catullus* (London: Routledge, 1996).

John Godwin (ed.): *Catullus: The Shorter Poems* (Warminster: Aris & Phillips, 1999).

————: *Catullus: Poems 61-68* (Warminster: Aris & Phillips, 1996).

G.P. Goold (ed.): *Catullus* (London: Duckworth, 2001).

Richard Jenkyns: *Three Classical Poets: Sappho, Catullus & Juvenal* (London: Duckworth, 1982).

Brian A. Krostenko: *Cicero, Catullus and the Language of Social Performance* (Chicago & London: University of Chicago Press, 2001).

R.O.A.M. Lyne: *The Latin Love Poets from Catullus to Horace* (Oxford: Oxford University Press, 1980).

E.T. Merrill (ed.): *Catullus* (Boston: Ginn, 1893).

Charles Martin: *Catullus* (New Haven & London: Yale University Press, 1992).

Kenneth Quinn (ed.): *Catullus: The Poems* (Bristol: Bristol Classical Press, 1996).

Jesse Sheidlower (ed.): *The F*** Word: The Complete History of the Word In All Its Robust and Varied Uses* (London: Faber & Faber, 1999).

Craig A. Williams: *Roman Homosexuality: Ideologies of Masculinity in Classical Antiquity* (Oxford: Oxford University Press, 1999).

T.P. Wiseman: *Catullan Questions* (Leicester: Leicester University Press, 1969).

————: *Catullus and his World: A Reappraisal* (Cambridge: Cambridge University Press, 1985).